Kwakiutl Legends

Chief James Wallas

Kwakiutl Legends

as told to Pamela Whitaker
by Chief James Wallas

hancock
house

ISBN 0-88839-230-3
First Paperback Edition 1989
Copyright © 1989 James Wallace and Pamela Whitaker

Second Printing 1994

Cataloging in Publication Data
Wallace, James, 1907-
    Kwakiutl legends

    ISBN 0-88839-230-3

    1. Kwakiutl Indians—Legends.   2. Indians of North
America—British Columbia—Legends.   3. Kwakiutl
language.   I. Whitaker, Pamela.   II. Title.
E99.K9W34   398.2'09711   C81-091102-7

Published simultaneously in Canada and the United States by

HANCOCK HOUSE PUBLISHERS LTD.
19313 Zero Avenue, Surrey, B.C. V4P 1M7
(604) 538-1114   Fax (604) 538-2262

HANCOCK HOUSE PUBLISHERS
1431 Harrison Avenue, Box 959, Blaine, WA 98231-0959
(206) 354-6953   Fax (604) 538-2262

Table of Contents

Introduction
By Peter J. Wilson

The stories in this book relate the traditional tales which Mr. James Wallas has learned from his elders, who lived in Quatsino Sound and on Hope Island. Mr. Wallas's forefathers are members of a people known generally as the Kwakiutl, although the term is misleading because it originally referred to a sub-group living at Fort Rupert. The Kwakiutl inhabit an area which at present includes Campbell River at the southern extreme, Quatsino Sound at the western extreme, various inlets of mainland B.C. at the eastern extreme, and Smiths Inlet at the northern extreme. Traditionally, the Kwakiutl lived in villages located in this general area (excluding Campbell River and Cape Mudge) which were organized into tribes. Today, most of them live on reserves near towns, maintaining some remote villages for food preparation and preserving during the spring, summer and fall.

The language which the Kwakiutl speak is known as Kwak'wala. This language is a member of the Northern Wakashan Branch of the Wakashan Language Family, which extends from the tip of the Olympic Peninsula in Washington State to Kitimat, B.C. (see map). Kwak'wala is divided into five dialect centers:

Campbell River-Cape Mudge, Alert Bay-Fort Rupert, Quatsino, Hope Island, and Smiths Inlet-Blunden Harbour. The language is still used on and off reserves by adults and some children, even though almost everyone is able to speak English. Unfortunately, most young people do not speak Kwak'wala fluently. This has caused concern among many adults, and they have instituted second language instruction in several schools.

Kwak'wala was not formally written by the Kwakiutl until contact with European civilization. The only permanent records kept by the Kwakiutl were carved on totem poles which conveyed family history and crests. Following contact, many missionaries, educators, linguists, and Kwakiutl have written Kwak'wala using English or phonetic writing systems.

Mr. Wallas is from the Quatsino tribe which inhabits Quatsino Sound. According to Mr. Wallas, the Quatsino originally lived at Cash Creek (marked on the charts as Shuttleworth Bight). The Indian name of this location means "place where the Quatsino came from." Quite a long time ago the people living at Cash Creek split up, half going to the villages in Quatsino Sound, while the other half remained and from then on were known by a name which means "always stay in the same place." Eventually, this group left Cash Creek and joined with the tribe at Hope Island.

About the Author

James Wallas, or 'J.J.' (from Jimmy Jumbo) as his friends call him, was born March 15, 1907, at Bear Cove, the original site of Port Hardy. His father, also known as Jimmy Jumbo, was from a village of the Quatsino tribe on Quatsino Sound. Both Mr. Wallas's paternal grandparents were from the same village. His mother, Jeanny Jumbo, was from a village on Hope Island as were both her parents.

Prior to and at the time of his birth there were several villages along Quatsino Sound and its inlets. Mr. Wallas lived with his family in an old village at the top of the narrows, a site that was gradually becoming the amalgamation point of the various settlements.

During long winter nights, he learned most of his stories around the longhouse fires. "We had no newspapers or radios at that time," he smiles. "Usually four families would share a longhouse, one in each corner, each having their own fire. If only two families were in a dwelling they would often share a fire."

At about six to eight years of age, Wallas started learning the stories, mostly from his father's eldest brother. "He knew I was interested and used to invite me over to his fire for tea," he said. "There were not many in the tribe who were interested enough to learn the legends."

Mr. Wallas speaks nostalgically of summers spent at beautiful Hope Island where they used to fish for halibut. They stayed at the village of his mother's people where he heard many of the stories that he knows. All that is left there now are a few rotting corner posts, indiscernible in the tall grass. However, a rock that bears the marks of a people who measured the winter solstice stands on the point. "They used to be able to tell a lot about the weather for the coming year and the salmon runs by the way the sun hit that rock," Wallas explains.

Before he was married to Annie Charlie at nineteen years of age, 'J.J.' did much trapping of mink, raccoon and marten. "The land otter was too smart for me," he quips. After his marriage he worked for years on fishing boats—gillnetting, trolling, and as a skipper of a seine boat.

His first job with the white man was at a cannery at Quatsino. He later did some logging, and worked at the Port Alice Pulp Mill when, he can remember, they still used horses at the mill. During the Second World War he was a foreman there in charge of thirty-two men. In later years he did some halibut fishing. "It looks easy, but there's a lot of work in that," he comments.

His wife was a daughter of a chief whose village at Winter Harbour eventually amalgamated with that of Wallas. The couple have three children: Frank, the eldest, a fisherman, who is presently the chief councillor of the Quatsino Band; Mary, wife of Eli Hunt, also a fisherman; and Stanley, the youngest, skipper of the cruise ship *Cona Winds.* James and Annie Wallas have nineteen grandchildren and fifteen great-grandchildren.

Mr. Wallas has completed an Indian Education Teachers' Training program in Campbell River and presently teaches Indian Studies at the Coal Harbour elementary school.

In 1974 the people of the old village at Quatsino were moved to a new site near Coal Harbour so that schools, and medical and other services would be more accessible. At the old site, the less moveable structures remain, weathering in winter storms,

Below the inlet the tides continue to ebb and flow through Quatsino Narrows where canoes once traveled. Summer winds sweep through the ancient graveyard and sough through the Douglas firs that seem to stand guard over the old site. The trees whisper of times past when a strong and imaginative people gleaned their living from the sea.

Acknowledgments

We are very grateful to all our friends and associates whose help and advice made this work possible. They include Peter Kaweski, Campbell River District Superintendent of Education, Indian and Northern Affairs: Peter Wilson, linguist; Thelma Hals, proofreader; Dusty Cadwallader, deceased; and Peter Paterson.

Our thanks to the B.C. Provincial Museum for permission to use their photographs, and to the UBC Museum of Anthropology for the use of their masks to create the chapter dividers and cover.

Not least, we are grateful to our families for their unwavering encouragement.

Note to the Reader

James Wallas tells you these stories. He learned them when he was young and lived on Quatsino Sound. Some of these stories may be told in a little different way in other areas of the culturally rich Kwakiutl nation, but these are as Wallas learned them from his forefathers.

The beautiful old prayers included in this book are taken from Franz Boas's *The Religion of the Kwakiutl Indians,* Part II -Translations, Columbia University Press, 1930. They are not necessarily relevant to the stories which they accompany, but we feel they should be made available for the reader's enjoyment. Franz Boas worked with the Kwakiutl in the Fort Rupert area during the late 1800's and early 1900's.

Pamela M. Whitaker

1
Stories of Creation

Two-Headed Serpent

More than 2000 years ago, there were two brothers. The elder was the Transformer. They landed in Cape Scott and that's where it all began.

The Transformer said to his younger brother, Lone Man, "I must get you some food. I am going away to see that the job of creation is finished and it will be a long time before I return. Let us go to the point of the Island." So the two brothers went to the point of the Island. That is the very northern tip of Vancouver Island, at the Sand Neck, where there are long sandy beaches. Whales were swimming out in the water.

The Transformer took off Two-headed Serpent, his belt, and used it for a slingshot. Instead of using stones, he took the eyeballs from the belt to shoot at the whales. Now Two-headed Serpent had great power.

When the first whale was hit, it swam to shore and flipped itself right up onto the sand. The second one did the same, and so did the third. The fourth whale, a big blue whale, was the biggest of all, and when it threw itself up on the beach, the Transformer said to his younger brother, "You are going to be named for this, the biggest whale of all. You are going to be called *w'alus*—that means 'big.'"

Ts'igis, Monster
of the Deep

Ts'igis is like a giant bullhead with a long, long tongue. The word refers to the action of lying on the beach or in deep water, leering upwards.

The Transformer left his younger brother at Cape Scott and walked down the east coast of Vancouver Island to Cash Creek. That is where the Quatsino people lived at the time of creation. The village seemed to be deserted except for one boy.

"Hello there, young man," said the Transformer to the boy. "Why are you all alone and looking so lost?" He could see that others in the village had not been gone long as some of the houses still had lodge fires burning.

"There is just me and my Grandfather left," said the boy. The boy looked very thirsty.

The Transformer asked, "Where did the rest of the people go?" Then he pointed toward Cash Creek and said, "There is a good place to get water. Come and have a drink."

"I don't want a drink! I'm not thirsty," exclaimed the boy. "My grandmother says not to go there, because something is down in the deep part of the water. It is Ts'igis. Its tongue can go under the sand and every time someone goes near—not even all the way to the shore— the tongue takes him into its mouth!"

"Don't be afraid," admonished the Transformer. "Come on, you can get some water." He took off his belt, Two-headed Serpent, and put it around the boy's waist.

The boy said, "No! No! I'm scared! My mother was really thirsty and she went down there and now she's gone."

"You go and get some water," repeated the Transformer. "You don't have to be scared of that thing. You don't have to be scared." So the boy, with Two-headed Serpent around him, walked slowly toward the water carrying a bucket in his hand. Suddenly the creature's tongue came from under the sand and whisked the boy into its mouth.

The Transformer was not disturbed. He sat down and sang a little song, beating time with rocks that were on the beach.

Start the belt moving,
Start the belt moving.

In the monster's stomach the belt started moving. Soon the creature surfaced, swam to the beach and threw up the whole tribe. Some of the people were bones, some were just hanging together, and others were still fresh. The boy came out too. He was very happy and had the belt still around him.

The Transformer said to the boy, "With Two-headed Serpent you can help me put these bones together again. You think the people are dead, but they are only sleeping. Look—if you had refused to go near the water, you wouldn't have got your people back and you'd probably be dead too."

They started to assemble the bones. It was sometimes hard to fit the proper foot or arm to the right person or the proper head to the proper body. When the bones were all put together, the Transformer sprinkled them with the water of life and the people became themselves again. They started getting up, their eyes wild because they did not know what had happened to them.

"You've been inside that thing," said the Transformer, gesturing toward the creature on the beach. With that he grabbed Ts'igis by the neck and threw it as far as he could. "You are never coming back," he said. The people knew then that they were free of it.

Koskimo Dancer
Edward S. Curtis Photo

Mirrored
in Stone

Mr. Wallas says that when he was young he heard this story over and over again.

After the Transformer left the ancestors of the Quatsino people at Cash Creek, he continued down the east coast of Vancouver Island. It seemed that every person he was to meet knew that he was coming. In those days people sometimes knew things ahead of time— a spirit or something told them.

About three miles north of Shusharti Bay a man was looking into a pool of water on the beach. He looked at his reflection in the pool of water and prettied himself up. The Transformer came up noiselessly behind him and said, "How are you? What are you doing?"

The man did not look up. He just kept on smoothing his hair and fixing himself up. Then he answered, "I want to look good when the Transformer comes. I heard that he is coming and I want to look nice."

"Look! I am the Transformer," he said. "What did you want of me?"

The man did not believe him and kept grooming himself. The Transformer asked again, "What do you want of me?"

"I am just going to stand here and fix myself up for when the Transformer comes," replied the man.

"You will stand there forever," said the Transformer. The man was turned to stone, and the rock can still be seen leaning over the water north of Shusharti Bay.

Rat Fish

The Transformer continued his journey down the east coast of Vancouver Island till he got to Tsaxis, which today is called Beaver Harbour. It was a beautiful day—no clouds in the sky, no ripples on the water. There he saw a man standing in a canoe singing to the world about what a great man he was. "Don't let anybody near me," he sang. "I am the best of all and I don't care about anything."

The Transformer called to him from the beach, "Come on in. I want to talk to you." When the man came in to shore, the Transformer asked, "What are you doing? Why are you singing that song?"

"Oh, I'm just singing because it's a nice day and I'm bored," said the man, "No place to go, nothing to do."

"Well, what do you want to do? What do you want to be?" asked the Transformer.

"I don't care," replied the man.

So the Transformer turned him into a rat fish. "In that case, you are going to be a rat fish all your life." He picked him up and put him in the water. As the rat fish swam away, you could hear it singing:

> *Where's Knights Inlet?*
> *Where's Knights Inlet?*
> *Where's Knights Inlet?*
> *Where's Knights Inlet?*

Speaking Blind

There were two old ladies digging roots in a mud flat. They were blind. Without their knowing, the Transformer came near and watched them.

One lady said to the other, "I smell something awful." The other answered, "Don't talk like that. It is what we are digging."

"No," cried the first. "It is he that is supposed to be coming that smells bad." The women both laughed.

Just then the Transformer asked, "What are you doing?"

"Digging roots," the ladies replied.

"Do you want to see?" asked the Transformer. "Would you like to see a nice day? Look on a man's face?" He did not wait for an answer but made them both see.

One of the women exclaimed, "You must be the Great One!"

"Turn around the other way," advised the Transformer. He grabbed the women by the side, threw them up into the air and said, "You are going to be mallard ducks, feeding for the rest of your lives in the smelly mud."

Go Not Alone

"I am the greatest man of all," shouted one man as he picked up a rock and smashed it to the ground.

"No, I am greater than you," countered another as he too threw a rock with great force.

The Transformer came across these two men arguing and fighting and asked, "Why are you throwing rocks? What are you arguing about?"

"Oh, we're just killing time," said one.

"We're just killing time until the Transformer comes," said the other. "We heard he is coming and we want to see him."

"I am the one for whom you wait," said the Transformer. "Are there just two of you?"

"Yes," they answered.

"No wives?"

"No."

"You need companionship—that is why you are arguing," stated the Transformer. "You need someone to share your life with, someone you can talk to—a wife." He split each man into a male and female. "You go one way," the Transformer told one couple, "and you go the other."

The Nimpikish River

The Transformer started off again down the coast and had not gone far when he met a man standing all alone on a beach. He asked the man, "What do you want to do with your life? What do you want to be?"

"I want to be something to help my people," answered the man.

"Then how would you like to be a big cedar tree? Your people could weave mats and clothing from your bark and use your wood for their lodges."

"No, I don't want to just stand there. I want to help my people in another way."

"Would you like to be a big boulder?" asked the Transformer.

"No! That's worse than a tree and doesn't help my people much."

"How would you like to be a big salmon in the bay that your tribe could catch and eat?"

"No, I do not wish to be a salmon."

"How about a river? Then the salmon would swim up the river and your people could catch them easily and live on them."

"Yes, that would be fine," said the man. "I would like to be a big river." The man suddenly found himself falling backwards. The Transformer had put his hand on the man's forehead and given him a little push. When he hit the ground he became a mighty river—the Nimpkish.

The people were really happy then, because every summer lots of fish came up the river to spawn—Sockeye, Cohoe, Spring—all the best salmon. Later on there was a large camp located at that spot.

Prayer to
the Olachen

"Now welcome, fish, you who have come, brought by / the Chief of the World-Above that I see you again, / that I come to exert my privilege of being the first to string / you, fish. I mean this, that you may have mercy on me that I may see you again next year when you come back to this your happy place, / fish." *

Thus the prayer of a Kwakiutl woman as she strung a sharpened cedar stick through the left gills and mouths of the Olachen.

* Franz Boas, *The Religion of the Kwakiutl Indians,* II, page 203.

Masked Dancers
Edward S. Curtis Photo

Eulachon - The Strung Up Fish

At the time the Transformer created the eulachon, he had crossed over from Vancouver Island to Knights Inlet, a long winding inlet at the end of Queen Charlotte Strait. When he arrived at the top of the inlet he saw some people camped by the mouth of the river.

"What would you like to have come up your river?" he asked the people. "Would you like salmon to smoke? Would you like eulachon to make oil from?"

It was the end of the winter and the people were tired of dry salmon. "Eulachon!" they cried. "We would like eulachon for oil and to eat fresh."

So the Transformer took his blanket from around his shoulders and dipped one corner in the water of the river. Suddenly the river swarmed with little silver fish—eulachons.

The people feasted on fresh eulachons and dried some for the future. They made the rest into eulachon oil, storing the fresh oil in kelp bulbs.

It has been said the eulachon are so oily that if you light the end of a dried one it will burn like a candle.

Lone Beach - Roamer

The Transformer had been gone a long time. When he arrived back at Cape Scott, he found a pile of bones lying on the sand— human bones. They were his brother's.

He laughed and said, "My brother, you are not dead. You are only sleeping." He took some water of life and sprinkled it on the bones of Lone Man, and his brother stood up.

"I am going to leave you now," said the Transformer, "and I will not be back. You are to stay here. People will come to you, and you will be the ancestor of many generations."

When the Transformer left there, he probably went to Scott Island, because a big stone footprint is there. Another footprint is on Calvert Island, they say, so that shows you which way he must have gone.

The Deluge

Every coastal tribe seems to have a story of the Great Flood and each differs a little.

"The Bella Coola Indians say they put all their masks in a box to save them," said Mr. Wallas. "When the water rose to the top of the mountain, they tied up and put the masks out on top. The masks are still there turned to stone."

The tribes do not always agree as to which were of the original tribe and which are descendants of people that were in a canoe that broke away. According to Mr. Wallas, Cape Mudge Indians (from Quadra Island near Campbell River) and Neah Bay Indians (at the southeastern-most tip of British Columbia) are among those that say they broke away.

The Quatsino people that lived below the inlet knew the Flood was coming a long time before it happened. In those days they seemed to know some things ahead of time. Some of the people decided to go underground to a place where the water could not reach, but most of the people built strong canoes.

One of these canoes was larger than the others. It was the lead canoe. Using a long cedar withe rope made from twisted cedar bark, they attached a big rock anchor to the lead canoe. All the canoes were lashed together with poles between them. Lots of fresh water in wooden containers, and dried meat and fish, clams, and berries were stored on board.

One day when all the canoes were prepared, it started to rain hard. The people noticed that the water of the sound was rising above the high tide mark. Some families started getting into canoes; others went underground.

"I see a big wave coming," someone shouted, and they all looked and could see, in the distance, a mountain of water racing toward them. They moved fast then!

The flood hit, and the canoes rose level with the mountain tops across from their village. It was really rough up there. They tried to avoid huge trees that were rooted up. Pieces of their former homes dashed against the sides of their canoes. Some of the canoes broke away and were lost in the raging storm. The canoes that broke away later ended up in other places and started other tribes.

When the water started to recede and the tops of the mountains became dry land, the people would get out, stretch their legs, and have something to eat. Sometimes they would camp there for a few days. That is why fossilized clam shells have been found at the top of some mountains.

Finally the people could see their old village site again. Nothing was left. All their lodges were gone, their totem poles, even all their earth. But the people who had gone underground had survived. They came out one by one, happy to see the daylight, happy to breathe fresh air again.

"There is a lot of dirt underground," they told the people. So the chief instructed, "Each of you who has a basket, make several trips a day under the ground to bring up earth for our village site."

They did so, carrying the baskets on their sides. Soon there was more than enough earth on which to build the village, but a lot more had been spread at one end of the site than at the other. "You are going to have to smooth that out," the chief advised the people. They did as best they could, but the ground is still a little slanted there.

Then the chief announced, "I am going to try to find out if any of our people who broke away during the flood have survived." He climbed to the top of a hill, faced the north, and sent out his power, calling, "whoooooooooo." The sound echoed over the hills, but there was no answer. If there were any survivors in that direction, his power was not strong enough to reach them.

Then he faced the setting sun and called again—"whooooooooo." There was no answer from that direction either. When he sent out his power to the south, there was still no answer. He turned toward the mainland and called—"whooooooooo." Faintly, from a great distance away, was an answering call—"whooooooooo."

"It is from Kingcome Inlet!" shouted the chief. "It is our brother!" The people whose canoes had come to rest at Kingcome Inlet were happy, too, that their brothers had survived.

Epilogue

At Cape Scott, a few miles south of where the Transformer and his brother landed, there is a pile of big boulders. The Transformer had told the people that no one was to touch those rocks. "Do not kick them, hit them, or throw other rocks on them," he said. "If you do, a big storm will come up."

Now not more than one hundred years ago, some surveyors wanted to go to that place. They hired a man from Hope Island to be their guide. He was called George and had a canoe. When they arrived at that spot, George said to the surveyors, "Don't touch that pile of boulders. Don't kick them or do anything to them or a big wind will come up."

The men thought George was crazy to think that. "How can a pile of rocks bring on a big wind?" they scoffed.

George repeated the warning, "Don't touch those rocks or we will have a terrible storm," but the men paid no attention. They went over to the pile of boulders and kicked them and shouted at them. They picked up other rocks and smashed them down on the boulders.

George pulled his canoe off the beach and tied it down very securely in preparation for the big storm. He took his tent and pitched it deep in the shelter of some trees.

"Don't leave your tent on the beach," he advised the surveyors. But the men just laughed and paid no attention to him. They went to bed with their tent sitting out on the open beach.

Late that night the surveyors awakened to the whistling of the wind in the trees. Soon it became a howl, and rain pelted out of the black sky. A strong gust of wind ripped up their tent stakes and blew the tent high into a tree. Waves almost washed over them as they struggled against the wind to reach the shelter of the trees.

"George! George!" they shouted. "Can we come in your tent? Ours is up a tree!"

"I warned you and you wouldn't believe me," he answered. "Now you go up in the tree and get your tent down—I have no room,"

As he finished this story, Mr. Wallas gazed out the window in the direction of Hope Island where his mother was born. "George died only fifty years ago," he mused.

Prayer to the Sun /
When a Canoe Is Caught
in a Gale at Sea

"*Press down the sea in your world, Great Chief, Father, that it may become god, / that your world may become right on the water, Great Father,*" / *

* *The Religion of the Kwakiutl Indians,* II, page 183.

Prayer When a Canoe Meets a Rough Sea at a Steep Point (No'mas)

"*Look at me, Old Man, that the weather made by you may spare me; and, / pray, protect me that no evil may befall me while I am / traveling on this sea, Old Man, that I may arrive at the place to which I am going, Great Supernatural One, Old Man.*"—"*Hâ, it will be that way.*" *

* *The Religion of the Kwakiutl Indians,* II, page 189.

The Moon
Is Thirsty

It was a very dry time. There was not much water anywhere—not on the earth and not on the moon. Those camped beside the Nahwitti River on earth were fortunate.

The full moon looked down and saw the people camped there. "How lucky they are," he thought. He called down to them, "I am going to come down and get a drink of water."

The people all came out of their lodges to see the moon descend to the earth. He came down in slow diagonal sweeps. Each sweep was about a mile wide. He came closer and closer to where the people were, but could not land. He was too big to make the final sweep down to the Natwitti River. So the moon, still thirsty, went back to his place in the sky.

2

Thunderbird

The Thunderbird

"In the old days slavery was common," said Mr. Wallas. "There was more slave-taking than killing between tribes that lived not too far from each other. Slaves were desirable, not only for helping with the work, but also for bartering in trade. Sometimes a child slave would be given away at a potlatch and was considered a very valuable gift.

"I think they were well-treated. I remember meeting three slaves when I was young. Of course, they were pretty old by that time. I was really surprised when I found out they were slaves because the adults did not tell us—they didn't want the children to tease those people."

Slaves were not allowed to marry into the tribe by which they were captured. They were, however, permitted to marry other slaves. After years of service, they were quite often given their freedom but usually opted to stay with their captors.

The Thunderbird is a legendary, eagle-like bird, so big it could pick up whales in its claws. It told the ancestors of the people, "You will know I am around when you hear the thunder; it is the sound of my wings flapping. You will know I am around when you see the lightning coming from my blinking eyes. If you hear me during rough weather, the weather will change for the better. If you hear me during fair weather it will change for the worse."

Long before Port Alice appeared on South East Arm, or Neroutsos Inlet as they call it today, a thunderbird landed on Snow Saddle Mountain, which you can see from the Inlet. As a man, Thunderbird made his home on the flat at the head of the inlet where the pulp mill now stands.

One day two hunters from Quatsino passed by in a canoe and saw Thunderbird. They were surprised that anyone was living on the flat, and the man did not speak to them. The hunters did not know the stranger was a thunderbird. They went back to their village and told their people about seeing the stranger at the head of the inlet.

The chief said, "We don't want to share this inlet with anyone. We will take canoes and warriors and go and kill this man or bring him to our village as a slave."

One day some of the warriors took their canoes and went to the head of the inlet where the strange man had been seen. The Thunderbird did not hide but came out to speak to them. One of the warriors said to the stranger, "We have come to kill you, but if you wish to live you may come with us as a slave."

"I'll come with you," Thunderbird answered, "I would rather be a slave than die. But just wait while I get my things together. I will leave my wife and one daughter here, and take my other daughter with me."

He went into his lodge and brought out a box. His daughter brought a smaller box. "Don't worry," he said to his wife. "We'll be alright, because we will do just what they want us to do."

The canoe headed back down the sound toward Quatsino village. One warrior took his paddle and poked their captive. "I heard you are a thunderbird," he scoffed. "Why don't you fly?"

"Yes," said another brave, "why don't you take off and show us how you can fly?" You are nothing but a man like us. You're just ordinary."

Thunderbird did not answer. He did not say a word.

The warriors threatened, "You're going to

work hard for us because if you don't we are going to kill you."

Thunderbird answered quietly, "I will work hard for you and my daughter will help too."

But the braves continued to poke him with their paddles and taunt him. "Are you really a thunderbird?" they queried. "No, you're not a bird—just a man. If you were a thunderbird you would show us how you can fly. You've got no wings."

Thunderbird ignored them. "How far are we from your village?" he asked.

"Not far. Are you willing to work when you get there?"

"We will work hard for you," Thunderbird repeated. "My daughter will do the lighter chores and I will do the heavier. Tell me when we are almost at the village."

"We are coming around the point where the village is now," said one of the warriors, and they all began talking among themselves.

Thunderbird said, "Pass me that box my daughter brought." He took a blanket from the box and gave it to his daughter. "Here," he said, "wear this when you are a slave." He took a second blanket from the box and put it around her shoulders. "You might as well wear this one too," he added. "It will keep you warm when you are working outside."

He asked the warriors to pass the bigger box that he had brought and they handed it to him. He took from it a long feather coat and a huge, eagle-like head-dress. Quickly he put them on and leaped to the crosspiece of the canoe. "Get into my claw," he shouted to his daughter.

She did and Thunderbird began to grow bigger and bigger. He said to his daughter, "When we rise into the air, shake the top blanket. I will tell you when to shake the other."

Thunderbird ruffled his magnificent feathers and took off. The warriors sat immobile in astonishment. Higher and higher Thunderbird rose until he blotted out the sun. His mighty wings flapped, making a terrible sound like thunder, and the wind from them roughened the water. Lightning shot from his eyes.

The daughter shook the first blanket. The sky darkened and it began to hail. The men in the canoe continued to sit, frozen in fear.

"Shake the second blanket now," Thunderbird instructed his daughter. She did and the hailstones grew as big as rocks. These killed the warriors and sank their canoes.

Bridal party arrives for a potlach
Photo by Edward S. Curtis

Sport of the Thunderbirds

Before the time of confusion, when birds and animals all talked the same language, four big thunderbirds came down to the earth. They came to challenge the people of the earth to a little sport.

"We want to find out who is best with the spear," said the biggest of the four thunderbirds. "Tell your best spearman to get ready. Ours is waiting. We have a little bone here with a hole through the middle to toss into the air. You go first and if you miss—we win. If you spear the hole in the bone (it was about as big as a ten-cent piece), then you toss it up for us to try."

The people of the earth were excited at the prospect of the contest. They all turned to Kingfisher because they knew that none could surpass him in spearing fish.

"Will you represent us against the thunderbird?" they asked. Kingfisher was proud to accept.

Everyone gathered in a circle—a big circle with the thunderbirds and all the animals and birds in it. "You'd better give us lots of room," the thunderbirds warned. "Is your man ready?"

"Yes, I'm ready," shouted Kingfisher from the middle of the circle. A thunderbird tossed the little bone high in the air, and at the same time all four thunderbirds started flapping their wings. As Kingfisher streaked to the little target, thunder, lightning, wind, hail and rain assailed him.

"Jaa! Jaa! Jaa!" cried the little mink from his place in the circle down on the ground.

"What's wrong with you?" shouted his neighbor. He could barely hear his own voice in the great storm.

"The wind blew gravel in my eye," answered the mink.

By this time Kingfisher was blotted from sight, but when he flew back down he had the little bone on his spear. When the thunderbirds saw that, they stopped flapping their wings and the storm receded.

"Now it's your turn," the earth people chorused. "We are going to toss it to you now and see if your spearsman is as good as ours." And one took the little bone from the Kingfisher, and tossed it as far as he could.

As the little bone was tossed into the air, someone patted the crane's chest until all were enshrouded in a powdery fog. Those standing in the circle could barely see the person next to them.

"I've got it! I've got it!" shouted Thunderbird, and when the fog cleared the people could see he had the bone on his beak. The Thunderbird and Kingfisher were equal spearmen. It was a draw!

A Whale for the Thunderbird

In the days of which I speak, people did not have a chance to spear the whale, because of the thunderbird. He sat on top of a mountain looking over the Pacific Ocean. When he saw a whale, he would swoop down and take it for himself to eat.

One man had an idea. He said, "Let us all go together and get some second growth hemlock, heavy with sap, and make a wooden whale. We will need full-length hemlock," he told the people.

When the two sides of the whale were finished, they needed something to hold them together. Gwul'ik, whose name means pitch in the Kwakwala dialect, lived nearby. He was made of solid, clear pitch like that of the spruce.

'Gwul'ik, let's go out and fish for halibut," invited the man.

"No! I'm afraid of the sun," exclaimed Gwul'ik. "It might melt me before I come home again. I only go out before sunrise or after sunset."

But the man talked Gwul'ik into going halibut fishing. "We will leave tomorrow morning before daybreak," he said. "You can take a cover to protect yourself from the sun if it is too hot."

"Okay," agreed the pitchman. "I'll come— but don't stay out too long."

They went fishing early in the morning. Each had a fishing line. They had caught a few halibut when the man asked Gwul'ik, "How are you? Are you getting tired?"

"No, I'm alright," answered the pitchman.

The sun had risen. "Are you alright now?" asked the man.

"Oh, I'm okay," he said and put the cedar bark cover he had brought over his head.

When the sun had walked a little farther across the sky, the man asked again, "How are you, Gwul'ik?"

"I think we'd better go home now," the pitchman replied in a very weak voice.

So the man slowly started for shore. "How are you, Gwul'ik?" he repeated, but there was no answer. Gwul'ik was melting fast.

The pitch slowly started covering the floor of

the canoe. The man threw out the halibut they had caught to make room for it. Then it got so deep he had to bail it out.

When he reached shore, he called to the other people, "Come and help—there's lots of pitch here now."

They came with wooden buckets. There was lots of pitch to seal the home-made whale inside and out. They let the wooden whale set for a day or two, then put it in the water and tested it. It was watertight.

Then the man asked the grizzly bear, the black bear and the cougar to come. "Each of you bring a boulder inside the whale," he instructed. He asked some wasps to come too.

"I'm going too," cried the mink.

"What are you going to do if the big thunderbird comes after our home-made whale?" the man asked.

"Oh, I'm brave! I'm strong!," Mink assured him.

So the mink came along and he too brought as big a rock as he could carry. When the whale was launched, all the animals walked to the front end carrying their rocks and the whale's head submerged. When they walked to the tail end, the head came up and water spouted out of the blow hole.

The man in the wooden whale could see that the mighty thunderbird had left his perch and was circling the water. "When he grabs us," he

Koskimo Indians
Photo Credit: Provincial Museum, Victoria, B.C.

said to the wasps, "fly out and sting his eyes so he can't see." Then he said to the bears and the cougar, "You rip his stomach open with your powerful claws."

The great thunderbird swooped down and grabbed the wooden whale in its strong talons and started to lift it from the water. The wasps hit his eyes, and the bears and the cougar clawed his stomach.

The female thunderbird was watching from the mountain peak. "Don't move," she said to her little ones, "I think your father is in trouble." She flew down to him and picked up the whale and the male thunderbird. One of her claws pierced the wood and pinned Mink to the ceiling near the blow hole. He was caught by the corner of his eye and hung suspended.

"Jaa! Jaa! Jaa! " he cried in pain.

"We told you not to come," said the others. "You are just in the way.

They were being carried across the water toward the rocks and were all becoming alarmed.

The wasps swarmed out and stung the lady thunderbird on the eyes. Quickly the bears and the cougar finished her off, and she dropped them. They landed in the water not far from the rocky shore.

3

Mink

Kwakiutl Prayer to
the Sun at Sunrise

"Welcome, Great Chief, Father, as you come and show yourself this morning. / We come and meet alive. O protect me that nothing / evil may befall me this day, Chief, Great Father." *

* The Religion of the Kwakiutl Indians, II, pages 182-3.

Mink, Son of the Sunshine

The bright sun was shining on a village by the smooth sea. In her lodge a young maiden sat basking in a sunbeam that came through a slat. The slat was like a little window with a sliding door, the only window in the lodge.

The girl enjoyed warming herself in the rays of the sun. A few weeks later she found out she was going to have a baby and her parents questioned her about it. They asked her who the father was.

"I don't know any young men," their daughter replied, "and I stay home all the time. The only thing I can think of is that I was standing in that sunbeam warming myself."

The time came for the baby to be born. They named it Made-like-the-Sun, the Mink.

When the child was growing up, the other children used to make fun of him. "You

65

haven't got a dad," they would say. "You're not like us."

Made-like-the-Sun would come in crying to his mother. "Don't listen to them," she assured him. "You have a father."

"Where is my father?" asked Made-like-the-Sun.

"See that warm sun up there?" said his mother. "That is your father. Without him nothing down here could live."

"How can I get up there?" the boy wondered.

He noticed other children playing with bows and arrows. One day he asked his mother, "May I have a bow and arrow to play with so that I can learn to shoot?"

"Since your father is way up in the sky, I will ask your uncle to make you one," replied his mother.

The little mink longed to see his father. His uncle had made him a fine bow with four arrows, but he wished and wished that he could go up in the sky and see his father. One day he climbed a little hill away from where the other children were playing and shot an arrow high into the sky. It stuck up there! He shot a second arrow that stuck into the handle of the first. The handles started stretching back to earth. He shot a third arrow and it stuck into the second and stretched even farther back to earth. The fourth arrow, his last, did not quite reach the ground, so he took his bow and attached that. It reached the earth. He shook it hard and it became a cedar withe rope.

Made-like-the-Sun climbed up, up, into the sky. He did not tell his mother where he was going. When he got to the end of the rope, he walked and walked toward the setting sun. It was almost dark when he saw a house and went to the door. "Who are you?" he was asked.

"I am Mink, son of the sunshine," he replied.

"Come on in," he was told. "Your father, the sun, is inside. Soon he must walk again all day back to the west." The boy was taken into the presence of the brilliant sunshine.

"So you are my father," said the little mink, Made-like-the-Sun.

"Yes I am," replied the sun. "You have come at the right time," he continued. "I am not young any more. I am getting old and tired. Now I am going to instruct you to take over."

"You will walk from east to west, but you must not listen to the people down on earth. The people will say to you, 'Give us a little more sunshine so we can warm up. Clear the rain and clouds away,' but you must not listen. Just keep on walking from east to west. Do not stoop down, or there will be terrible fires below." He took off his sunshine mask and gave it to his son. "Tomorrow morning I will be with you to show you the way."

Early the next morning, Made-like-the-Sun rose in the east with his sunshine mask on. He was the great sun! His father accompanied him as he walked across the sky toward the west. He did very well. When the people on earth called up to him, "Give us more sun," he did not listen. He just kept on walking.

But the next day when he traveled alone across the sky, he was not so strong. At first he tried to be. He heard the people down below saying, "Let the sun shine a little more to clear these clouds away and warm us up."

"No," he said, and kept plodding from east to west. But he kept hearing people calling him from below. "We just want a little more sunshine—just a little more to warm us up."

Finally he said, "I'll give you just a little more sunshine," and he stooped down a bit. Then the people began complaining about the heat. The forests began drying out and the rocks on the shoreline cracked.

Father Sun heard the people screaming down on the earth. "Oh, it's too hot! We're going to burn up!" and he went to see what his son was doing.

There Made-like-the-Sun was, stooping down. The Sun grabbed the mink by the neck and pulled him back. "I told you not to stoop down. I told you to keep walking," he thundered. "I will take my job back now," and he flung his son back to earth.

Made-like-the-Sun landed in the water in a magnificent dive. That is why the mink is a skilled diver like his mother the sea lion.

Mink's Search for a Wife

One day Made-like-the-Sun, the mink, went to his mother's home on some rocks in the channel. "I'm old enough to get married now and there is a girl that I want to marry," he told her. "I've never seen a girl like her before. She has long, dark brown hair that goes to the ground. She's really nice."

"If you think she is the girl for you, then marry her," his mother said.

So Made-like-the-Sun and the long-haired girl were married by the chief of the village. The mink suggested to his bride, "Let's go out in the sea. It looks like fun out there."

"It's too early yet," replied the girl. "Too early. Let's wait for a while."

A little later the mink asked again, "Let's go out there now. It looks like a lot of fun."

"Okay," she said, "we can go out now, it is

almost low tide." So the mink and his bride went out in the water. The girl ran her foot down to the floor of the sea and hung on with her toes. She leaned her body in the direction of the tide, and her long, brown hair streamed out on top of the water.

"When the tide is going out you lean out to sea," said the kelp girl to her husband. "When it is coming in you lean toward land." The mink was not aware that he had married a kelp girl.

"Yes," said Made-like-the-Sun, "but let's go down under the water for a while. Let's submerge."

"The tide will soon make us submerge," replied the girl. "It is getting stronger and stronger."

Sure enough, when the tide got higher they went under the water. The kelp girl clung to the bottom and also to her husband. Pretty soon Mink got short of breath. He gasped to his wife, "Let us go up on the surface."

"No, we can't do that. We have to wait until the tide goes out again."

"I can't take it any more. I can't wait that long," cried Mink. "I'm going to drown!" He wriggled in his wife's grasp. She let him go and he rose to the surface. Mink just lay there bobbing on the water, foam coming from his mouth and nose.

His brother found him there and took him to

their mother's house. "Mother, I think I am married to the wrong girl," Mink said when he had opened his eyes. "She's a nice-looking girl, but I almost drowned. You almost lost me."

"Yes," agreed his mother, "you made a mistake."

The next day the mink again went to his mother and said, "Mother, I have found a nice girl."

"Who is it this time?" asked the mother.

"She's a young girl with a little round face. A really nice girl. I want to marry her."

"Well, don't blame me if you make another mistake. But maybe this time it will be alright," his mother sighed.

So the next day there was another wedding in the village. This time Made-like-the-Sun married the frog girl. He was anxious to get out in the pond with her.

"When are we going to go out?" he asked. "When are we going to go out and make a noise in the pond?"

"We must wait until the sun moves a little more toward the west," his wife told him.

"But I can't wait," he cried. "Let us go now. I want to get out there and start croaking."

"You had better wait," she said. "The big bull-frog has to croak the first croak, then all the other voices can join in."

Finally the evening sun indicated the time to go out to the pond. It was a small, round pool of water, not much bigger than the top of a table. All the frogs went into the pond and sat with just their mouths sticking out of the water. Mink and his wife crouched in the pool and hung on to each other, waiting for the big bull-frog to make the first croak.

When the chorus began, Mink really enjoyed it. But then the noise began to bother his ears. Suddenly he could not stand it any more. "Let me go," he cried. "You people make too much noise!"

He broke away and ran to his mother's house. "Mother," he said, "do you hear that noise? My wife is out there. I think I have married the wrong girl again."

Only a day later, the mink approached his mother again and said, "Now I think I've found the right girl for sure. She's a nice, quiet girl who doesn't say much. She's nice-looking too."

"Okay, you may get married again, but I hope this is the last time," said the mother. "You are keeping our people busy marrying you every day."

After the wedding, Made-like-the-Sun moved into the house where his wife lived. She was nice and quiet—didn't say a word. When Mink started getting hungry, he waited for his wife to make something to eat, but she did not move. Finally he asked, "When are you going to cook something to eat?" There was no answer. He asked again. "When are you going to make something to eat?" but still she did not answer. He asked her again and again, but she would not answer him.

"I just want to know when we are going to eat. Why don't you answer me?" he cried. Her silence infuriated him. He shouted, "I am going to punch you in the nose if you don't answer me." His quiet wife did not say a word, so he punched her in the nose with his fist. Blood appeared on her face. "Look at you now," he stormed. "You've got a bloody nose and it is what you deserve."

Mink felt something on his hand and looked down and saw that his hand was bleeding. It had broken open when he hit his wife on the nose. He was married to a boulder!

The fourth time Mink wanted to get married, he said to his mother, "I think I have found the right girl for me. This girl looks really nice. She walks up in the air. I would like to walk up there with her."

So Made-like-the-Sun got married to a cloud. He went up in the sky with her and said, "Let us go for a run."

"We have to wait till the wind comes," she replied. "Can you run fast?"

"Sure I can run fast," said Mink. They did not wait long before a southeast wind came up. Mink was happy then. Those southeasterners can really make the clouds move fast.

The wind rose. Mink had to run faster and faster to keep up with his wife. He started to fall behind. She looked back and said, "Can you run a little faster? The wind is really strong now."

Mink tried but could not keep up to the cloud. Finally he lost track of her and gave up.

He went home to his mother's and said, "Mother, my wife is gone. I could not catch her. She runs too fast for me."

"So, you have taken the wrong girl again," said his mother. "Maybe you had better stay single."

When Made-like-the-Sun came once again to his mother's home wanting permission to be married, he said, "I have found a girl that will be the final one. She is a nice, decent girl."

"I hope this is the right girl and you will stop getting married," admonished his mother. "It's too much work for the chief."

So the mink got married again. A few days later, he told his mother, "I am married for the last time. This is the girl I want. This is *Gwalus.*" In the Kwakwala dialect, this word also means "the final time." He seemed to be happy married to a lizard.

Captives

Years and years ago, man and all the other animals spoke the same language. That was before the time of confusion.

Warriors attacked a village where many lived. They captured Made-like-the-Sun, the mink, and Land Otter, and others for slaves. The canoe with the captives in it was heading down the inlet when Mink said to the warrior who was paddling, "Why don't you sing a song about capturing us while we are on our way back to your village?"

"Maybe I will—but why don't you sing a song first?" the man answered.

"Okay," said Made-like-the-Sun, "but only if you will act out what my song says."

His captors agreed to do that, so the mink began his song.

Go along the shoreline
And when you see where trees are
Hanging over the water,
Paddle under the trees.

That is how the mink's song began. All the people joined in the song because it was part of the fun.

Go close to the beach now,
Go close to the beach now.

"That is a good song. We have never heard it before," said one of the warriors admiringly. "You're good at making songs."

"Paddle under the tree now," said Mink, and they paddled under a tree. Suddenly Made-like-the-Sun jumped up on the overhanging tree and was gone.

The land otter continued to sing while this happened. "Let the mink go," said one. "We won't miss him too much. We still have the otter and the others."

They all started singing again, "Go along the shoreline." The land otter was looking down in the water as he sang. "Go close to the beach now," they sang. The otter waited until he saw a codfish, dove in the water, grabbed the cod and swam under the canoe to shore. He streaked into the woods with the fish in his mouth.

The men in the canoe were angry. "We won't use this song any more," they cried. "We have lost two slaves now. Let us keep the others that are left."

Mink's Meal

Harbor seals are always fat when they are young. They are so fat and juicy, the mink wants to eat them.

One morning the mink went to the home of a baby seal and asked its mother, "Can your son come out and play with me?"

"No, he can't," the mother replied. "He's too fat. He has so much blubber he can't walk. He can only roll around." The baby seal's head was sticking out of his fat like a small balloon.

The next day the mink went to the seal's home again and asked if the baby seal could come out to play. The mother said, "No."

The third day, the mink said to the mother seal, "If you allow your son to come out and play with me, we can roll around on the ground—we can find a nice smooth spot." The mother did not let her son go out that day, but the next time the mink asked, she did.

"I think I will let you go out now," she said to her son. "But don't stay out too long. Come back when you get tired and lie down for a while."

Mink was really happy then. His mouth began to water for the taste of the tender baby seal. He and the baby went out to play. They rolled around on the ground for a while, then they saw a smooth, gentle slope. "You do what I do," instructed the mink, and he rolled down the slope. The baby seal rolled down the slope too.

Then the mink saw a smooth, little hill. "Can you make it up that hill?" he asked the seal.

"Sure I can," replied the baby, and they both went to the top of the hill.

"Remember to do what I do," said the Mink. "When you get to the bottom of the hill, shut your eyes and rest for a while." The mink rolled to the bottom of the little hill. He lay at the bottom with his eyes closed for a few minutes. Then he got up and called to the little seal, "You can roll down now."

The little seal rolled over and over down the hill. When he reached the bottom he closed his eyes for a few seconds, then opened them wide.

"You opened your eyes too soon," cried the mink angrily. Then he reminded the seal in a softer tone, "You need your rest."

Mink climbed up the hill again and when he had rolled down to the bottom he closed his eyes for quite a while. Then he said, getting up, "Now it's your turn."

The baby seal rolled down the hill again and this time when he reached the bottom he kept his eyes shut a long time—long enough for the mink to find a big stick and kill him with it.

The mother seal was worried when her little one did not come home that night. She asked her neighbors, "Have you seen my son anywhere? He was playing with a mink."

"I saw the mink dragging something to his house," one of her neighbors informed her.

The seal went to the mink's house and demanded, "Where is my son?"

"Oh, when I finished playing with him I left him outside and went to my home," lied the mink.

"Well, he didn't come home," stated the mother seal.

She asked every person she met, "Have you seen my son? Have you seen my son?" Then someone told her he had seen the mink cutting up some meat and cooking it. She knew then that her son would not return.

Raven

The Raven's Cry

The four cousins of the raven—Crow, Blue Jay, Slug and Spawn Ball, the spawn of the Ling Cod—put up a lot of berries for the long stormy winter. They smoked and dried clams, too, while the weather was still fair. These were some of the favorite foods of Gwaw'ina, the raven.

The raven found out that his cousins had a lot of food stored for the winter and suggested, "Why don't we take some of the food and donate it to the chiefs of the villages down the inlet. It would be a gesture for peace."

His cousins agreed that it would be a good idea. So they packed a borrowed canoe with preserved berries and clams, and set out. Raven sat at the back of the canoe while his four cousins paddled.

They had gone a long way from home when Raven said to the ladies, "Could you pull into shore? I want to get out for a little while."

"Okay," agreed his cousins, and they brought the canoe into the beach. They all got out except Raven.

"I'm just going to go around the point and take a look. I'll be right back," he said. As soon as Raven got out of his cousins' sight, he disguised his voice to sound like many warriors approaching. It was an ominous sound. Then he returned to where his cousins were waiting on the beach and asked, "Did you hear what I heard?"

"Yes, we heard it," his worried cousins answered. They all climbed back in the canoe. "What do you think," they asked. "Should we go home?"

"We've come this far—there's no sense in going back," replied Raven. "You ladies go and hide in the woods. I'll wait here for the warriors. They won't harm me if they think I am all alone."

So the crow, the blue jay, and the spawn ball all climbed back out of the canoe and went to hide. The slug could not move very fast. She was very, very slow.

"You'd better hurry," cried Raven.

"I'm trying," answered Slug, as she slowly inched her way up the side of the canoe.

Raven impatiently grabbed the slug and

threw her out of the canoe. Then he started to eat the berries and clams as fast as he could.

Slug looked back and saw what Raven was doing. She called the others and they all came from their hiding places. They grabbed their paddles and beat the raven with them until he cried, "Gwa-gwa-gwa!" That means "Don't! Don't! Don't!"

Prayer to Berries

*"I have come, Supernatural Ones, you, Long-Life-Makers, that I may take you, / for that is the reason why you have come, brought by your creator, that you may come and satisfy / me; you, Supernatural Ones; and this, that you do not / blame me for what I do to you when I set fire to you the way it is done / by my root (ancestor) who set fire to you in his manner when you get old on the ground that you may bear much fruit. Look! / I come now dressed with my large basket and my small basket that you / may go into it, Healing-Woman; you, Supernatural Ones. I mean this, that you may not be evilly disposed towards me, friends. That you may only treat me well," / says she. / ***

* The Religion of the Kwakiutl Indians, II, page 203.

They Laugh at Raven

In one big village lived families of bear, deer, ravens, kingfishers, sparrows and others. It was a time when there was not much to do.

"How shall we pass the time?" the people of the village wondered.

"Let's get the families together and sing and eat," suggested Raven.

"Sure," said Kingfisher, "that's a good idea. Let's start tomorrow. You can all come to my place."

So Kingfisher got his fine spear ready. He went down to the river and out to the end of a long tree that hung over the water.

"Oh boy," the people thought as they watched. "Maybe we'll have a salmon feast."

Kingfisher could see a shape under the water, moving up river. He struck, embedding his sharp spear into the fish behind its gill. He brought the salmon out and soon had two more.

The next day the people all came to his home for the feast. They were very happy, laughing, singing and eating. Then one asked, "Who is going to be next?"

"That's me," said Raven. "I'm going to be next. May I borrow your spear in the morning?" he asked the kingfisher.

"I don't know....," said Kingfisher. "It's a really good spear—the only one I've got. You might break it if you miss a salmon and hit the rocks on the river bottom."

"Oh, I won't do that," Raven assured him. "I'm good at spearing salmon. I will be very careful with it."

So the next morning Kingfisher lent his spear to Raven. Raven went out on the same tree hanging over the water that Kingfisher had fished from. He waited till he saw a large salmon swimming up the river, then drove the spear as hard as he could. It pierced the salmon close to its tail and the big fish pulled Raven into the water. "Help! Help!" he cried.

The people gathered on the river bank to watch. Raven did not let go of the spear because he did not want to lose it. Someone went into the water finally and pulled him out. He was a mess of wet feathers.

"Why did he do that?" the people questioned. "He's not good at spearing fish."

Sparrow said, "I'll give the next feast. Come to my place tomorrow." The people wondered what the little bird could give them.

The next day Sparrow asked the people to help him bring berry bushes into his house. There were no berries left on the branches. When lots of bushes were stuck into the dirt floor and all the people had gathered, the little bird sat on one of the limbs and started to sing a beautiful song. Suddenly berries came out on all the bushes—fat berries that looked like clumps of fresh salmon roe. They were salmonberries and enough for all the people.

The guests were enjoying themselves very much. They asked one another, "Who will be next?"

"I'm next," shouted the raven.

"What are you going to give us?"

"Salmonberries, just like the sparrow," retorted Raven.

So they all went again to Raven's house where Raven had got his helpers to stick a bunch of bushes into the floor just like the sparrow had. They watched as he tried to sit on one of the branches. He was so heavy the bush wobbled. It could hardly hold him. Raven started whistling and trying to sing like a sparrow. One or two blossoms came out on the bush and only one half-rotten berry.

"He's always imitating someone," exclaimed

the guests as they turned their backs on him in disgust.

The next day they were all invited to the deer's home for a nice roast of venison. The raven would not go. He was thinking about his past two failures and how all the people laughed at him.

"Come on, Raven," they called.

"No, I won't," Raven sulked, but then he smelled the delicious meat cooking and changed his mind.

"It's too late now," he was informed, "but if you want some meat, you can stick your beak through that knot-hole and we will give your some."

So he put his mouth through the knot-hole. They gave him a strip of meat. It was wrapped around a small stone that had been heated red hot in the fire.

"Gwa-gwa-gwa!" cried Raven when he tried to gobble it down. Then he flew away.

But when all the people had gathered the next day at Harbor Seal's house, Raven was there too. The harbor seal had made a big fire in his house and lined up several wooden pots beside it. He bathed and stood close to the fire, holding his hands to the flame. Oil started dripping from his fingers into the pots and, when they were all filled, he divided the oil among the people.

"Who is going to provide the feast to-morrow?" the guests asked as they were happily leaving for home with their good oil.

"I am! I am!" shouted the raven.

"What? What are you going to give us this time?" the people queried, but the raven did not answer.

The next day the raven built a big fire in his home. Then he bathed in the river. He looked strange with his feathers dripping with water. He held his feet to the hot fire, but only one drop of oil came out. You could hear his skin cracking. That is why Raven has such rough skin on his feet today.

"Why do you try to do what everybody else does?" the people asked. "Why don't you do something of your own?"

"Tomorrow you will have salal berries from me," stated the bear to those assembled. They all turned to look at him.

"Where will he get them?" they asked one another. All the bushes around camp had been stripped.

The next day the bear bathed thoroughly. When the people came to his home he asked the biggest of all his brothers to come and slap him on the backside as hard as he could. The biggest bear gave him a mighty whack and all the wooden pots were filled to the brim with salal berries—nice clean berries with no stems on them.

Of course the raven tried to copy the bear. He too bathed in the river and assembled some wooden pots. Then he asked a bear to smack him on the bottom.

Smack—and the raven went tumbling across the room. All that came out was some dirt. The people went home, laughing again at the raven.

Water for the Earth

A long, long time ago there was no water anywhere—no creeks, no lakes. The only drinking water people had was water that dripped from roots.

Now Raven was very thirsty. He knew a place at Bull Harbour where there was water. So he went to the house of the lady who had collected the water from dripping roots. He carried a stick in his hand and asked, "May I come in and get a little fire with this stick so I can cook my breakfast?"

"Yes, come in," said the lady.

When he was inside, Raven looked around and saw the bowl of water in a corner. "My mouth is awfully dry," he stated. "Do you think I could have a sip of your water?"

"Yes, but don't take too much," replied the lady.

Raven went to the corner and started drinking from the rock bowl. He was gulping it down as fast as he could when the lady cried, "What are you doing? I need that water for myself."

Raven stopped drinking and walked over to the fire. He bent down, pretending to get fire on his stick and quickly put some ashes in his mouth. Then he turned to the lady and said, "Look at my tongue—my mouth is still very dry. Can I have just one more sip of your water?"

The lady peered at his dry-looking mouth. "Okay," she agreed, "but just take a little." She got her cooking pot and busied herself at the fire.

Raven started drinking again from the rock bowl as fast as he could. By the time the lady saw what he was doing the water was all gone. She grabbed the stick that Raven had left by the fire and went after him with it. He escaped out the door and flew away.

As Raven flew over the parched land, water dripped from his beak—a drop here and a drop there. Where one drop fell, a creek or lake appeared. Two drops fell at once as he passed over the lower mainland and formed the mighty Fraser River. Where three drops fell, the Columbia River started to flow.

Crow and Raven

"I will be back in about one hour," Lady Crow told her children. She walked down to the beach and started digging for clams with her yew-wood digging stick. Soon there was a pool of water where she was working.

A curious little harbor seal surfaced in the sea near her. "Why don't you come a little closer?" invited the lady crow.

So the little seal submerged, then came up closer to where the crow was digging. "Why don't you come up here into the pool that my clam digging has made?" asked the crow.

So finally the little seal did come right into the pool the crow had made and she killed him with her digging stick. She tipped over the clam basket, put the seal in it, then covered him over with clams. She set off for home thinking, "I will call my relatives to come and share this delicious feast."

Raven was sitting outside his house as Crow walked by. Now Raven has very sharp eyesight and a keen sense of smell. "What have you got in that basket?" he called.

"Oh, just clams," said Lady Crow.

"No, you've got something in there besides clams," admonished Raven. But the crow ignored him and walked to her home. She cooked the clams, then started cooking the seal.

A neighbor of the crow was out for a walk and strolled by where the raven was sitting. "My," he said to the raven, "that crow is really lucky—she got a harbor seal and clams too."

"I knew I could smell meat cooking," exclaimed the raven. He wondered, "How am I going to get some of that delicious food?" Then he thought of something. He called over a little boy who was playing nearby. "Run from one end of the village to the other and yell, "So and so's house is on fire!" he said to the little boy.

The little boy did what Raven asked. Everybody, including the crow, heard him yelling that so and so's house was on fire. Crow dropped her cooking and rushed to the other end of the village where she thought the fire was.

Raven moved fast. He went into Crow's house and started gobbling up her food.

"You had better get home quick." someone

said to Lady Crow. "Raven is eating your cooking."

Lady Crow rushed home and found the Raven had eaten half the clams and part of the baby seal. She picked up her digging stick and beat Raven with it as hard as she could. He said, "Gwa-gwa-gwa," as he flew away.

Kwakiutl Wolf Dish
Photo Courtesy B.C. Provincial Museum

5

Deer

Turning the Tide

At the time of this occurrence, the wolf was in control of the tide. He always kept it at high water mark. The people that lived near Shusharti Bay could not dig for clams or take mussels from the rocks. It was winter and their salmon and berry supply was getting low. Hunger stalked the village.

The winter winds blew strong. The people were crouched around warm fires in their lodges. "I don't know how we're going to get the wolf to change the tide for us," they said to one another.

Then the deer spoke. "I have an idea," he said. "I have an idea. We are all hungry. Everyone in the village is hungry. So this is my plan. I am going to pretend I am dead. Put me in a box and I will have with me the sharpest mussel-shell knife you've got. Tomorrow you can mourn me. Say, 'The deer is dead now. He had been hungry for a long time.' Then you will see what I will do.''

The next day the people spread the story, "The big buck deer has died of hunger. He starved to death.'' They made him a cedar box held together with pegs made with strong wood from the yew tree. The deer got in the box, and the people carried it to the edge of the clearing. The clearing was close enough to the village so that the people could see if Deer needed help. They left the cover of the box open about seven centimeters on one side, then went back to their doorways to watch.

The wolf was hungry too. It was not long before rumor reached him that Deer had died. He went to investigate and the scent brought him to the box that Deer was in. The deer heard the big wolf outside and his little heart went tic-tic-tic.

Wolf sniffed around the box. "It smells like a deer in there,'' he said to himself. "Oh boy, this will be my supper.''

Now the wolf used his tail instead of his paws for some things, and he pushed his tail through the narrow opening and felt with it all around the inside of the box.

"There's a deer in there alright,'' he was thinking, when quickly Deer sliced off the wolf's tail in one clean stroke. Wolf was so shocked he ran home as fast as he could go. He was disappointed that he had missed such a satisfying meal.

Deer climbed out of the box and took the wolf's tail back to the village. "The wolf will be back for his tail," he announced, holding it up for all to see. Then he hung it over the fire.

It was not long before a lone wolf came into the village and appeared at the door of the deer's house. "I have come for the tail of my brother," he stated.

"Before we give you your brother's tail, you must make us a promise," the deer answered. "We want you to let the tide go out so that we can dig clams."

Wolf thought for a while, then replied, "We will let the tide go down so that you can get mussels off the rocks."

"We cannot live only on mussels," the deer replied. "We want clams." He lowered the bushy wolf's tail a little toward the fire. The fire leaped at the tail but did not quite reach it. The tail started becoming black from the smoke.

Wolf ran back to the pack and told his brother what the deer had said. Soon he was back. "We will let the tide out for one day so that you can have a good feed of clams," he said. "Then we will bring it back to the high water mark."

"We don't want to have the tide out for just one day," retorted the deer, lowering the wolf tail a little closer to the flames. "We want it to go out every day." The smell of singed fur filled the lodge.

Wolf hurried off again. It was not long before he was back. "My brother, the leader of the wolves, whose tail it is you have, said that in return for his tail we will allow the tide to go out twice a day. Every six hours it will change."

The villagers were happy then. Deer returned the blackened tail, and the wolf disappeared into the forest. He could hear some of the people shouting after him, "If you break your promise you will all get your tails cut off." After that there was plenty of food in the village.

How the People Got the Fire

A long, long time ago when there were no matches, only one person in the world had fire. He would not share it with anyone. He would not even let the people take a little on a stick.

The man who had the fire was very powerful and the people were afraid to try to get some fire from him. One day the deer said, "Don't worry—we will have fire. I can run fast. With my swiftness I will get fire and give some to everyone. I want you all to gather in a circle at the door of the man who has the fire, and sing. You can sing for me while I dance in the middle of the circle."

The deer took two strips of pink pitchwood from the fir tree and hung them around his ears. They looked like decorations for his dance. The people began to sing, and Deer danced in the circle. The man who had the fire came out of his lodge to listen and watch. Deer danced in the middle, then slowly around the edge of the circle. Then he slipped through the crowd and into the man's lodge.

Quickly he caught the pitchwood that had been hanging around his ears on fire, then touched it to the black hair inside his knees. He slipped out through the crowd and ran as fast as he could back to the village. The man who had the fire saw him streak away but could not catch him.

That is why the black hair inside the deer's legs smells like pitch smoke. Deer did good work for his people.

Drifting

A deer and her fawn were chased by cougars. The mother was caught, but while the cougars devoured her the little fawn got away. Blindly it ran and ran until it came out on a beach where a man was making a canoe.

The man worked alone. Nearby he had a small canoe. It was during the time that animals and men spoke the same language.

"Spotted One, why do you run so fast?" asked the man.

"I'm running from my enemy, the cougar," replied Fawn. "They caught my mother and ate her. I don't want them to get me!"

"You can use my small canoe," offered the man. "Not far from here is the Kyuquot village. Why don't you leave it there for me?"

"It would make me very happy to use your

canoe so I can get away from Cougar," said the little fawn.

The man gave him his paddle and the little deer got in the canoe and gratefully paddled away. A mist came up. The fawn paddled till he was tired, then drifted for a while, then paddled some more.

He sang a little song.

I'd like to know
Where I'm going to end up
Where I will drift.

The little fawn was very tired and hungry. He drifted a long, long time. Then the canoe touched bottom. He was on a beach. He got out of the canoe and looked around and felt the sand. "I think this is Kyuquot," he said to himself. And it was.

6

Other
Animal Tales

The Big Elk and the
Little Brown Bird

*According to Mr. Wallas, the little brown
wren in this story is about the size of a thumb and
can be heard singing in the summer.*

One day the magnificent elk was walking
down his own trail when he met a little brown
wren. "Could you move to one side so I can
pass you and go where I want to go?" asked the
wren.

"No, I won't," said the elk. "I'm not going to
move for a little bird like you."

Wren made up his mind he was going to
make the big elk move, so he jumped on the
elk's front hoofs, first on one hoof, then on the
other. Elk tried to stamp on the little wren but
was not fast enough. He was getting angry.

The little wren continued to tease the elk,
"You're too big. You're too clumsy. You're
too slow. You can't catch me," he railed.

Elk stamped down hard with one of his hoofs but missed again. "I'm going to sniff you right into my nose if you don't stop that," cried the elk. He put his head down and snorted in hard. Now the elk has very wide nostrils and the little bird went right through him and out the back door.

Wren flitted around to the front of the elk again and started singing a song:

Where did I come through from you?
You know you took me through your nose
But where did I come out?

Everything inside you is open,
So I came right through you
And out the other end!

"You stop that singing or I'll sniff you into my nose again," shouted Elk, and he tried to strike the bird and crush him to the ground. He missed, so he bent his head down and sniffed the bird once more into his nose.

The little bird went right through the elk's body and out the back door again. He came out singing his song:

Which way did I come out?
You know you took me through your
*   nose.*
I did not come out your mouth.
I did not come out your ears.
I came out the other end!

Elk was furious. Wren could see that he was going to be sniffed up the elk's nose a third time, so he quickly gathered up some dry twigs in his beak. Elk sniffed a great sniff and Wren found himself once again in the elk's body. Instead of going right out the back door, the little bird sat down and rubbed two twigs together until they started to burn. He added the other twigs to them and took off his little cedar bark cape. The cape was soft and dry and quickly caught the flame when he put it on the fire. He then went out the back door of the elk. This time he did not sing his song.

It was not long before the elk started to cough, and every time he coughed smoke came out of his nose and mouth. Elk coughed harder and harder. The smoke coming out of his nose and eyes became thicker. Then the big animal fell over and died.

Wren did not go where he was headed in the first place. He went back to the village and sang to his mother:

> Tell everyone to go where the elk is,
> Tell them to sharpen their knives,
> Tell them to gather their baskets.
> The elk is on the trail
> Where I killed him.

"How did you kill him?" asked his mother. "You are so small and the elk is so big!"

The little wren told his mother what had happened. "See, Mother," he said, "my cedar bark cape is gone."

"I am going to send someone with you to see the elk before I tell the people," she said. "They might be mad at me if you are not telling the truth."

A woman from the village went with Wren, and he showed her the elk lying on the trail. "It is true. There is a big elk out there," she reported to Wren's mother when they had returned.

So the whole community readied itself to go out and butcher the big elk. They sharpened their knives and gathered all their different kinds of baskets. Some carried meat to their homes in baskets with handles, and other carried it in baskets strapped to their backs.

An old lady who could hardly walk was the last one on the trail. "You'd better hurry or there won't be any meat left," she was told by those she met returning with their meat.

When she reached the remains of the elk, only one man was there, putting away his knife. "Is there any left?" asked the old woman.

"No, nothing. You're too late. There is no meat left," answered the man.

"I'll take anything," said the old lady. So the man gave her the guts, and nothing of the elk was wasted.

How the Eagle Got Sharp Eyes

In a village where a lot of people lived, someone had to look out for war canoes. The eagle was the only one that could fly to the top of a tall tree, the best place for a lookout.

Eagle's eyesight was not very good. He could hardly see anything, especially toward dark. He said to the snail (that creature commonly called a slug in the Pacific Northwest), "May I borrow your eyes?"

"No! I don't want to pull my eyes out," exclaimed the snail.

"Well," Eagle argued, "I've got to look out for war canoes from up in the tree. I want to be able to see them far away, so I can warn my people."

"Alright," the snail finally agreed, "as long as you bring them back to me when your job is finished. I'll use yours while you have mine."

Now the snail used to have exceptionally good eyesight. Snails used to be able to see plainly even a long distance away. So the eagle talked him into exchanging eyes. The snail gave his eyes to the eagle, and the eagle gave his eyes to the snail.

Eagle flew to the top of the highest tree. "My," he said, "these eyes I've got now are really good! I can see far, far away."

He sat in the tree and sat some more, looking all around. Then he made a noise (you know the noise that eagles make when they spot a bear or something unusual—he made that noise). Then he flew down and told the chief that there was a canoe approaching, although it was still a long way down the channel. Then he flew back up in the tree again.

He watched the canoe come closer and flew back down again to tell the chief, "You'd better prepare now. It's a war canoe. They're coming to fight."

"Very good!" said the chief. "You're a good man and must have excellent eyesight to be able to see so well."

Later on when the trouble was over, Eagle came down from his perch on top of the tall tree. Snail was waiting for him. "I want my eyesight back now," he said.

But the eagle replied, "I have decided to keep these eyes. They are much better than the ones I had before." And that is why the snail moves so slowly today.

Prayer to a Beaver after It Has Been Killed

"Welcome, friend, Throwing-down-in-One-Day, you Tree-Feller, for you have agreed to come to me. The reason why I wished to / catch you is that you may give me your ability to work / that I may be like you; for nothing is impossible for you to work at, / friend, you, Throwing-down-in-One-Day, you Tree-Feller, you Owner-of-the-Weather. / And also that nothing evil may befall me in what I am doing, friend," says he. *

* *The Religion of the Kwakiutl Indians,* II, pages 196-7.

The Beaver and
the Flea

It was very dry weather. A beaver was working, while a flea watched him.

"What are you making?" asked the flea.

"I'm making a dam," replied the beaver. "There's no rain, so I'm going to dam this little stream and make a pond." He finished cutting down an alder sapling with his big front teeth. "Why do you ask?" he inquired.

"Oh, I just wanted to know. I've never seen a dam before," answered the flea.

"I wonder when it's going to rain?" the beaver mused. "Nobody seems to know," he added, "so I'm going to make a house in the pond. When it does rain, I will have a home to go to."

"It never rains here," the flea informed him.

"It will some day," Beaver said.

"Then I should look for shelter too," stated the flea, "because if it should happen to rain I don't want to drown."

"Why don't you make a shelter like mine?" asked Beaver.

"Do you think I have time?" queried the flea.

"Sure." said Beaver. "There's no sign of rain yet—no clouds or anything. If you can't get your shelter finished in time, you can come into my hair and have shelter there."

It was not long before rain came. The beaver said to the flea, "It's too late to finish your shelter now. Come on, jump into my hair and I'll take you into my house."

"Okay," said the flea, "here I come," and he jumped into the beaver's fur.

When Beaver got inside his shelter, he started to itch. "You can come out of my fur now," he said to the flea, but Flea did not come out. He liked it in the beaver's fur. Beaver shook and scratched, and shook some more. Finally the little flea fell out, but the beaver did not see where Flea went.

Prayer to the
Black Bear

"*Thank you, friend, that you did not make me walk about in vain. / Now you have come to take mercy on me so that I obtain game, that I / may inherit your power of getting easily with your hands the salmon that you catch. / Now I will press my right hand against your left hand,*" says the man as he takes hold of the / left paw of the bear. He says, "*O, friend, now we / press together our working hands that you may give over to me your / power of getting everything easily with your hands, friend.*" *

* *The Religion of the Kwakiutl Indians,* II, pages 193-4.

The Black Bear

Two boys had gone up the river to gaff salmon with sharpened roots of yew-wood, when a bear started following them. Every time they caught a salmon and threw it to the bank, Black Bear would eat it. He was eating the fish as fast as the boys could catch them.

The boys were getting angrier and angrier with the bear. Finally they started taunting him, "Black Bear, you are stupid," they shouted. "You don't cook your fish like us. You just eat it raw. How can you eat it like that? Don't you know how to cook? You are stupid."

They went home and told their parents what had happened at the river. They said that they had called the bear names.

A few days later the boys were hunting with their bows and arrows and they spotted the same bear near the river. One boy shot at it.

The arrow reached its target, but Black Bear did not drop. He headed up river for a way and then into the deep forest. The boys followed through tangled bush hoping to get their arrow back.

Black Bear seemed to be weakening. He went slower and slower and finally came to a stop beside a big cedar root. The boys thought he was about to drop, but when they caught up to him the bear leaned down and picked up the huge root. It covered the entrance to a deep cavern.

"Come into my den," Black Bear growled, and he took the arrow from himself and gave it back to the children.

The boys were afraid then, but tried not to show it. They went into the den of Black Bear and could see, by the dim light, an old, old bear sitting at the back of the cave. He was very big.

"Sit down," said the grandfather bear to the boys. "You are the two from the river that called my son names. You sit down," he repeated.

The boys sat down near the fire where salmon was cooking.

"You are the ones," continued the old bear, "who said to my son at the river, 'You don't cook your fish—you are stupid. You just eat it raw. You don't know how to cook. Black Bear is stupid.' Well," continued the old bear, "we catch fish and eat them raw but we cook them too. We cook salmon and you're going to have some now."

The younger bear went to the fire, took some hot salmon roe and smacked each boy across the eyes with it. "See," he said, "we cook our salmon!"

The boys' eyes stung and they trembled with fear.

"Now you may eat some," invited the bears, but the boys noticed that the bears were not eating. They thought there might be something wrong with it.

The older boy whispered to the younger, "Let's not eat any." "No thanks," he said aloud, "we've got to get home. Our eyes are swollen and we can't see very well. We've got to go home. Our parents will be worried."

"Lift up the root and let them go," ordered the grandfather bear.

When the boys reached home, their parents listened to their story. The father of one of the boys suggested, "When you shot the bear with the arrow, Black Bear was just pretending to be badly wounded so you would follow him."

The villagers were unhappy that the bears had taken the boys into their den. "We must teach them a lesson," they agreed, and a massive bear hunt was held. As many bears as they could find were hunted down and killed.

But that night brought retaliation. When the

people were sleeping, bears swarmed over the village, wrecking their smokehouse, chewing up canoes, and scattering food caches. After that the people of the village thought it was better to live at peace with Black Bear.

Don't Make Dogs Fight!

The boys of the village liked to make dogs fight. One would say to the other, "Our dog can beat your dog anytime."

"No it can't," the other would counter. "This dog is a much better fighter!"

On and on it would go until the dogs were pitted against each other in battle. Both animals would come out of it ripped and torn. Nothing was gained.

One day one of the boys who liked the dogs to fight was out walking. He had gone a long way and was getting hungry when he met a strange man. "You look hungry," said the stranger to the boy. "Would you like something to eat?"

"Yes, I am hungry," said the boy, and he accepted the man's offer of hospitality.

The man led the way. As soon as the boy went through the door of the man's home, he saw several dog hides lying around the room. His host went immediately over to a big gray and black hide and picked it up. He turned to the boy and said, "When we put these on we become dogs. When we take them off we are men again."

The boy was speechless. He stood staring at the strange man and the dog hides.

"We don't like it when you make us fight," continued the man. "Our sharp teeth hurt each other. We get torn and bruised and sore, and sometimes we even break a leg or lose an eye."

The boy was so shocked he stood still in the middle of the room staring at the dog man.

"Sit down and have some food," invited the man. "Sit down."

The boy sat down. He was given a fine meal and he told the man that it was good. When he was about to leave, the man warned him, "You must never tell anyone about coming here or what you saw today. Not even your parents. Tell no one about what I told you."

"I give you my promise," said the boy.

The boy's family was eating when he returned to his village, but he told his parents that he was not hungry.

"Why aren't you hungry?" his mother asked. "You haven't eaten all day have you?"

"No," said the boy.

"Are you getting sick?" queried his father.

"No, I'm just not hungry," answered the boy.

"Then you must have eaten something. Did you stop somewhere and eat?" The questions kept coming, and finally the boy broke his promise to the dog man. He told his parents what had happened that afternoon.

It was not long before the boy started feeling weak. He became weaker and weaker, and even though he ate, his flesh began to shrink. His bones started sticking out of his body. There was nothing anyone could do to help him and he died.

Since that time, Indian children have been told not to make dogs fight.

Kwakiutl
Edward S. Curtis Photo

7

Salmon

Prayer to
the Salmon

"We have come to meet alive, Swimmer. Do not feel wrong about what I / have done to you, friend Swimmer, for that is the reason why you come that I may spear you, that I may eat you, Supernatural One, you, Long-Life-Giver, / you, Swimmer. Now protect us, (me) and my / wife, that we may keep well, that nothing may be difficult for us / that we wish to get from you, Rich-Maker-Woman. Now / call after you your father and your mother and uncles and aunts and elder brothers and sisters to come to me also, you, / Swimmers, you Satiater," says he. *

* The Religion of the Kwakiutl Indians, **II**, page 207.

A Salmon Story

A powerful man, one who knew how to make plans, once lived at the top of a cliff on Nigei Island. He had a wonderful canoe. The canoe would become the size that he needed, either large enough to carry a hundred people or small enough to take just a few. He could dip his paddle into the water and say where he wanted to go, pull the paddle once, and the canoe would be there.

Many people resented the man who could make plans because he was different from themselves, so he lived alone with his family at the top of the cliff. On the rock face of the island, there was an opening through which he used to climb to escape his enemies. The opening led into a passageway and to the top of the cliff where there was a smaller hole to come out of. At the bottom of the embankment stood a pillar of stone and, farther down, another on which Planner's great canoe rested.

Planner had a son who was of the age to be married. He did not want his son to marry an ordinary girl. He wanted a union that would help provide food for his people, who were often hungry.

The powerful man had heard of a type of fish called "salmon" that dwelled at the other side of the world. He said to his people, who lived down below the cliff, "I want my son to marry the salmon girl who is far across the water. We will take my canoe and go to where the salmon are."

The people did not know where he was going but they all climbed into the great canoe. Planner headed toward the open sea and put his paddle in the water. "Take us where the salmon are," he said, and gave the paddle one strong pull. The canoe with all the people in it moved as fast as lightning across the water to the other side of the world.

At the edge of the water of the strange place were big bins teeming with fish of different kinds. "They must be the salmon of which we have heard," the people said to one another in wonder.

Planner asked to speak to the chief of the nearby village and was invited into his lodge. He discussed with the man the possibility of marriage between his son and the chief's daughter.

"We do not have salmon where we come from," Planner explained. "Sometimes our people are very hungry. If your daughter marries my son, we would like her to bring salmon with her."

The chief looked at Planner. He looked out at the magnificent canoe and replied, "Yes, my daughter may marry your son and she will bring salmon. But before you go you must stay for a feast. It will be many days before the salmon reach Vancouver Island. During the feast we will teach you how to cook and preserve fish."

So a great wedding feast that lasted four days was held. The planner and his people tried all the different kinds of salmon. They learned how to prepare it and how to tell one kind from another. They ate the mild flesh of the small, spotted Pink, and the redder meat of the large Cohoe. They tried speckled-sided Chum and were surprised at the size of the delicious Spring salmon.

"One Spring salmon will feed many," the people exclaimed to one another. But their favorite was the rich red meat of the slim, silvery-blue Sockeye.

The guests learned many ways to cook salmon. They were taught how to smoke it and dry it for the winter and how to barbecue it. When they were preparing the salmon, they were instructed to leave the head on the end of the backbone so that the salmon would come alive again.

"When you barbecue salmon over a fire, there is a hole that you put the stick through," they were told. "Be careful that you don't drop any bones of salmon through that little hole or something will be missing when that salmon comes alive again—a fin or tail or something like that."

"You may throw the bones of the salmon into the water or anywhere else and they will come back again the next year. But do not drop them through the hole where the barbecue stick goes."

The chief of the village said to the planner, "When a child is born to our children who have just married, it will have a dance all its own— The Salmon Dance." He did the dance to show him how it went. "When twins are born, they too will have this dance, for twins are children of the salmon."

"There's another thing you must remember," added the chief. "When the salmon are coming up the river, no one should mourn. Even if someone dies at that time, do not allow your people to mourn or the salmon may cease to come up your river."

After four days of feasting and learning, the people of Nigei Island climbed back in the wonderful canoe. The son of the planner and his bride, the salmon girl, were with them. The salmon followed the canoe across the ocean to the shore of Nigei Island.

Planner stood up in the canoe and said to the salmon, "This is where the planner lives." The fish all spread out behind the canoe, jumping and splashing in the water. Each group was given a river of Vancouver Island in which to spawn.

8

Whales and Whaling

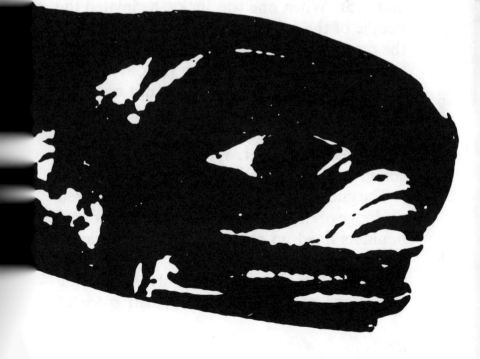

How Whaling
Got Started

The chiefs of two neighboring villages were rival hunters. Each hunted for deer, elk, seal and bear. When one was lucky, he invited the people of the other village to come and share the meat.

The chief of the village by the old sawmill across the water from Quatsino did not have the good luck that the Quatsino chief had. One day the unlucky chief was on a long hunting trip on Holberg Inlet. While he was gone, his son invited the Quatsino village over.

The guests beached their canoes and entered the lodge of the absent chief. They saw a row of boulders lined up on the floor and wondered what the boulders were for.

When they were comfortably seated the chief's son gave them each a small piece of dried salmon and eulachon grease in which to dip it. Then he said, "These boulders represent our river. I give you this river so you can have plenty of salmon."

At the end of the day, his father returned from Holberg Inlet, tired and hungry. He had had no luck hunting. His wife put some food in front of him and then she said, "Listen, while you were gone our son invited the people from the other village over and gave them some food. He told them they can use our river. They are going to come here and take all the salmon they want!"

The unlucky hunter pushed his food away. He did not want to part with their river. He hurt inside too bad to eat. He went to bed but could not sleep, so got up in the night and slipped quietly out of the house. He walked along the dark river wondering what to do. Should he do away with himself? What should he do?

When he came to a small lake, he sat down beside it and lost himself in thought. Dawn was coming, and with it the familiar noises of the awakening forest, when a strange sound disturbed his thinking—a blowing sound from the lake. Again he heard it, farther away. Then again he heard the sound, closely followed by another—an echo.

He strained his eyes in the early light and

seemed to see a slight movement on the water of the lake. A third time the blowing noise and its echo sounded. This time he could clearly see ripples on the water. "It sounds like a big whale," he thought. "But it couldn't be—not on a lake!"

Then he saw something in the water that looked like a stick. No, it was a tiny whale the size of a snail. It was hard to believe something so small could make so much noise.

The chief threw sticks at the little whale till it was washed onto shore. Then he scooped it up in his hands with some water. That was the last thing he remembered for a few minutes except for a voice in his head.

You are going to be a whaler,
You are going to harpoon the whale.
You are going to use this little whale;
Cut it open, dry it, attach it to your
harpoon head.

When the chief became himself again and returned to his village he called his people together. He explained to them how his son had given away their river and told them what had occurred at the lake.

"Now," he said, "I want you to get the biggest cedar tree you can find. Make a canoe out of it. Not an ordinary canoe, but one big enough and strong enough to carry a lot of people. Some of you hunters go for hair seal.

Skin them and make the skins into floats. Also, make a tank to hold some fresh water."

He instructed others to make harpoons out of strong, supple yew-wood with shafts about three meters long and mussel shell heads. The razor-sharp mussel shell was fitted onto a deer prong and smoothed over with pitch. It was tied to the shaft with a whale sinew leader and the harpoon shaft attached to the canoe with a cedar withe rope.

"When all is ready we are going after the big blue, grey or finback whale," the chief announced.

Several whalers left the village one morning in the early mist. They moved along Quatsino Sound in their large dugout canoe. The chief sat at the head of the canoe with the little whale dried and attached to his harpoon head.

Not far from Kains Island where the lighthouse is now, they saw a movement in the water. They pulled closer—it was a *K'ulis,* a big, blue whale.

The chief's harpoon easily found its mark behind the whale's front flipper. They were careful to keep the canoe to one side of its mighty tail so they would not capsize.

When the great whale weakened, the others quickly finished him off with their lances. The sealskin floats kept him from sinking.

The tide was too low to tow K'ulis up on

their beach, so they tied him to a rock at Drake Island (called Limestone Island in those days). At high water when they brought it home, their people were very happy and excited.

Each received a piece of whale meat the size of his hand to the depth of the whalebone. Then the people of the village across the water were invited over to feast on what was left.

Whalers Lost

The chief whaler of the village was a man of distinction. He owned his own large canoe dug out of a giant cedar tree.

One day he said, "The food supply of our village is getting low. We must prepare to go whaling."

Several men were anxious to go with him. They packed water in the canoe, but no food. Their equipment was made ready.

The whalers moved down the channel toward the open sea. They looked for the blue, grey or finback whale but would not take the sperm or killer whale that they could not use.

Soon Bulgina, a small grey whale, was spotted. The chief whaler thrust his harpoon and it imbedded itself deep behind the whale's front flipper. The creature blew out a mighty gust of water from his blow hole and started to submerge.

The whale moved off, going deeper and deeper into the water as it went. Sealskin floats had been attached to the line to impede the whale's progress and to prevent him from sinking when he died. They would let the whale tow them until it tired, then finish it off with lances.

But the whale did not seem to tire. It towed them out to the open sea. Although it was pulling a heavy load, it moved very fast.

"It must be the biggest grey I have every harpooned," exclaimed the chief whaler.

The whale pulled them all day and all night without slowing his pace. The men dreamed about getting home to the feast that would be awaiting them. After the feast each member of their families would receive chunks of whale meat the size of his hand cut to the depth of the whale's backbone. They thought about how good the strips of blubber would taste smoked and boiled.

For four more days the whale pulled them out to sea. It was getting weaker but so were they. Finally they cut the rope because they were afraid they would not be able to find their way back.

They paddled a long, long time in the direction they had come from. Day seemed to blend into night. Then they saw the shore of Vancouver Island.

But they could not find the channel that led to their village. Weakness overcame them. They pulled into shore and got out of the canoe and lay on the ground, where they perished.

Whale Island

A long time ago Solander Island, just off
Cape Cook, was alive. It was K'ulis, a big blue
whale. It stayed around Brooks Peninsula, not
far from two Indian villages. One village was at
Klaskish, which means "a place that is outside,"
and the other was near Ououkinsh Inlet. Both
the villages claimed the whale was theirs.

Men from one village would get a line on that
big whale and tow it right up to their beach.
When they woke up in the morning, it would be
gone. The other tribe had stolen up in the night
and towed it to their beach.

This went on for quite a while till the chief of
the Klaskish people said, "So that the others
don't get the whale, take our heaviest line, tie it
around the whale's head, and put an anchor on
it so that the whale will sink."

The men got the biggest rock they could take between two canoes, a line stretching from the rock to each canoe. When they reached the whale, they attached the rock to a strong rope that had been tied around the whale's head. Then they cut the lines to the canoes, and K'ulis sank.

"That's all we want," said the chief. "Now the other tribe can't take the whale away." They headed back to shore.

Not far from there, K'ulis came up again. He rose right out of the water, gave one mighty blow, and turned to stone.

A cry went through the village. "Come and look! There's a big rock out in the water!"

The Klaskish were happy then. "Even the island is ours," they said smugly, "because it is facing toward our village."

Killer Whale
Takes a Wife

A man had four daughters. The eldest was eighteen. Every day the girls walked on the beach to a sandy point where they liked to sit and look at the sea.

One day some killer whales went by while the girls were sitting on the point. The eldest girl said, "I am going to talk to those whales."

"No, you had better not," advised a younger sister.

But the girl did not listen to her sister. She called to the whales, "Killer Whale, come on in. We want a ride." The next thing they knew, a killer whale was right up on the beach.

"Do you think you know how to use this canoe?" he asked.

"I'd sure like to try," answered the eighteen-year-old girl.

"Come on in then," said the whale and opened his big mouth. The girl went through his mouth and into his body. He showed her the interior of his tail and fins and how to use them. He took her for a ride in the water.

"This is fun," cried the girl as they skimmed across the waves and down through the deep water.

When they came back to shore the whale said, "How about your sisters? Would they like a ride?"

"It's lots of fun," the oldest girl called to her sisters. "Why don't you try it?"

The second sister was not interested. The third sister would not try it either, but the youngest said, "I'm going to try it."

She went through the whale's mouth and into his interior but could not move his parts properly. Killer Whale said to her, "Go and tell your older sister to come and try it again."

So the eldest girl went inside the killer whale. They swam away and did not return. The three younger girls waited a long time, then went home and told their mother what had happened. "How are we going to get her back?" the mother wondered.

When the father heard what had happened, he took his canoe and searched out on the water. He looked for many days for his daughter but could not find her.

One day after he had given up the search, one of his younger daughters was walking on the beach. Her lost sister swam up to her and said, "Go and tell my parents I am married now to the killer whale." She was never seen again.

A Koskimo House
Edward S. Curtis Photo

9

Giant of the Woods

Big Figure

There were no schools in the days of which I speak, but there was a spot near the forest, a playground, where children used to play. One little boy that played there had a knife—what kind I don't know; it happened a long, long time ago.

The other children wanted to borrow that knife but the boy told them, "My mother and father won't allow me to lend it. My mother said you might cut yourself with it, then blame me. My father said you might lose it and never return it. That is what my parents told me."

Well, you know what kids are like. The children decided they would not play with the little boy with the knife. "Let him go by himself," they said to one another. They taunted the boy and teased him. Their backs were to the forest.

Suddenly the boy with the knife cried, "Hey! I see a big figure in the trees!"

The children did not turn around and look but kept their backs to the forest. "You're just saying that because we won't play with you," they shouted.

"No, I'm not," argued the boy. "There it is again! A big figure. It's watching us."

But the children would not listen. "You're just trying to fool us but it won't work," they chided. "We're not going to have anything to do with you."

"It's coming!" screamed the boy. "It's coming!"

The children saw it then. It was a big, big man, bigger than any other. He had hair all over his body and his eyes were set deep in his face. He carried a large basket on his back. The children's strength drained out of them in fear. They were helpless.

The woods giant grabbed the boy that had the knife first and threw him in his basket. Then he threw all the rest of the children on top of him. He set off through the forest while the children peeked through the cracks of the basket, trying to see where he was taking them.

The boy with the knife was right at the bottom of the basket and could hardly move with all the children on top of him. Finally he was able to cut a slit in the basket big enough to

squeeze through and he dropped to the ground.
The man did not notice, and the boy ran back
to his village crying, "Big Figure has taken all
the children!"

The men of the village gathered together.
They asked the boy to lead the way that Big
Figure had gone. They traveled over roots and
under logs. At the place the boy had fallen
through the basket the trail became harder to
follow. They could see where something big
had gone through the bush and followed that
till eventually the trail ended at a large cave.

The men of the village could dimly see some
of their children hanging by the feet in the dark
cave. A huge figure of a man was tying up the
other children's feet and putting pitch in their
eyes. His wife and children were helping him.

"What are you doing with our children?" the
villagers cried.

"We're going to smoke them," answered the
giant.

"Those are our children! We want to take
them home with us," said the villagers.

"We're going to smoke them and eat them,"
replied the big man. He and his wife finished
tying the children's feet and started hanging
them up, one by one, with the other children.

"Don't do that," the fathers of the children
pleaded. "Let us take them home with us."

The big man started building a fire under the

children. Then he said to the men, "Why are your faces so nice and smooth and not rough like mine? You have nice eyes. They don't sink way in your head like mine do."

The villagers thought fast. One of them said, "You can have a face just like ours. We can fix you up. Go outside and get a big flat rock and another smaller rock with a sharp end."

So the big man did what they asked. It was easy for him to carry the big flat rock because he was so strong. Then the men of the village said to the giant, "Lie down and use this flat rock for a pillow. We're going to fix you up just like us."

"How long will it take?" he asked as he lay down and put his head on the flat stone.

"Just four days," they answered. "Close your eyes. Close your eyes tight." Then they took the rock with the sharp end and sunk it between the big man's eyes. He was dead.

"How long is he going to lie there?" asked the giant's wife.

"Oh, about four days," answered the men. They took their children, untied their legs and removed the pitch from their eyes. Then they went home to their village where the people were very happy.

Big Figure and the Smoked Salmon

A family was camped by a river so that they could put up salmon for the winter. The salmon they had caught were hanging in a split cedar smokehouse.

One day before he went to bed with his family in the shelter they had made, the eldest boy went into the smokehouse and noticed some gaps between the fish that were hanging there. "Some of our smoked salmon seems to be missing," he told his father.

"We're the only ones here," his father replied. "Our family is camped all alone. Just forget about it—we'll get some more."

The next morning when the boy built the fire in the smokehouse, he noticed even more of the smoked salmon was missing. "Tonight I am going to hide in the smokehouse and find out who it is that is taking the salmon," he announced. "I will have my bow and arrow with me, but if it is a man that comes I will not use it."

That night they did not bank the fire very high and it soon burned out. The boy hid in a corner of the dark smokehouse and waited. Except for the rush of the wind in the cedar trees and the voice of the river, the camp was quiet.

It was not long before the boy heard a new sound—footsteps. Heavy footsteps were approaching the camp. They came closer and closer and stopped just outside the smokehouse. The boy was frightened but he had his bow and arrow ready.

Slowly the roof of the smokehouse lifted up. The boy pulled his bowstring taut. He dimly saw a huge hairy arm reach in toward the salmon and sent his arrow where the arm was coming from.

There was a terrible cry that woke up the others. "I think I got it! I think it's the woods giant!" shouted the boy to his parents. "Let's go after him."

"We will wait till morning," said his father. "He will be a lot easier to trail in the daylight and if you wounded him he might be dead by then."

The family rose early the next morning. The boy, his father and younger brother headed out on the trail of the giant. The trail they found had a few drops of blood on it. It led deep into the forest and ended at a cedar bark house. A pool of fresh water was nearby with a tree leaning over it.

"You wait here," the father said to his elder son, "and your brother and I will skirt around the back of the house."

While he was waiting, the elder boy climbed up the tree, as it was a good place to see from. Soon a large hairy girl came out of the cedar bark house with a bucket in her hand and walked to the pool of water that the tree leaned over.

When she stooped to scoop up some drinking water, she saw the boy's reflection in the pool. "My, I didn't know how pretty I was," she exclaimed. "I'm different from the rest of my family. Their eyes all sink in their heads and mine don't. They are hairy and I have smooth skin."

The boy above her moved in the tree, and a branch broke and fell to the water. The girl jerked her head up and saw him. "Oh, it is you that I see in the water," she cried. Then she paused and added, "My father has been terribly sick since he came home last night. Can you come and help him?"

"I'll get my father," the boy answered. "This must be where the person lives who was stealing fish from us," he said when he reached his father and brother. "I think he is very sick from my arrow. His daughter wants us to help him."

"Okay," said the father, "let us go in."

They went in the cedar bark house and a big hairy man more than six feet tall lay almost dead with an arrow deep in his chest. His wife and children were standing around him.

The boy who shot the arrow walked up to the big man and tried to pull the arrow out. It would not come out straight, and he had to twist it this way and that way. Finally it pulled free.

"I feel better already," said the giant weakly. "You have helped me, so I will give my daughter to one of you to marry."

"No!" cried the elder boy. "I do not wish to marry your daughter."

"I do not wish to marry your daughter either," exclaimed the younger son.

"Have you another offer then?" asked the father of the two boys.

"Yes, my offer is this. You may use us on your totem pole and face mask. No one else can make our likeness, only you. You can make the mask just like our face."

The father and his sons accepted the giant's offer and went home. They took their arrow with them.

No one else had a mask like theirs. It was a frightening mask with the eyes sunk deep in the head.

Big Figure's Wife

One day, Hunter was deep in the wilderness hunting for deer, elk or young bear when he heard a noise that sounded like someone working with an adze.

"That sounds like a canoe maker," he thought, "But who would be working this far back in the woods?" He knew that it was no one from his village.

Hunter moved noiselessly toward the sound of the worker, and it led him to a clearing where a big figure was hollowing out a large cedar tree with an adze. Her back was to him, but he could see that it was a huge figure of a woman. Her baby was seated behind her in the hollowed-out tree.

Hunter did not wish to startle the giantess, so he crept up to the back of the canoe and pinched the baby's little toe. The infant cried out. Without turning around the mother said, "That could be Hunter, who pinches you—the one who hunts on water and on land."

The hunter pinched the baby's toe again and it started to cry. "It's just that hunter teasing you, don't cry," said the giantess again without turning.

Finally the hunter came around to the front of the woods giant's woman. "Yes, it is I," he said. "What are you making that canoe for?"

"We live beside a long lake," said the giantess. "We will use it there. Why have you come to me?" she asked him.

"I followed the sound of your adze," he replied, "and now I have found you I want something from you."

"What is it that you want?"

"I am a provider of food for my people and I have not had much luck lately in hunting. Can you help me?"

"I will help you," responded the lady. "I will use my power to bring elk, deer and bear to you. When you are hunting in the water, seal will come to you."

The hunter was pleased at the big woman's generosity, yet he asked her for one more favor. "I want to use your features in a dance mask," he said.

"If you use me, you must use all of me and

my four children too," she replied. "This baby is the youngest of the four. You may use us all in a dance."

After that the hunter became a very successful provider of food, and a dance was created showing the huge woman with her four babies being born one by one.

Big Figure and
the Limpets

There were four or five children laughing and having fun on a beach. Their parents had taken a canoe and gone to a good place for digging clams.

The children were playing on the sand near a pit in which they had built a fire. They put rocks in the fire and, when the rocks were red hot, they baked limpets on them and ate them. The little limpet shells fitted perfectly on the children's fingers, and they were having fun playing with them.

At first they did not notice a big figure creep slowly out of the woods and advance on one of the children. It looked like a big, big man with sunken eyes and covered with hair.

Finally one child spotted him but made no outward indication that he had noticed. He whispered to the others, "It's Big Figure. Don't scream, don't run away. Pretend you are not afraid."

All the children put limpet shells on their fingertips and circled around to the other side of the huge figure so they were between him and the forest. The giant turned toward them, his back to the fire. The children were trembling but the eldest bravely said, "We are ones that can scare people too." They opened and closed their fingers as if they were blinking. Slowly they advanced on the giant, continuing to blink their fingers with the limpet shells on the tips. Big Figure started backing up as the children advanced. He took several steps and suddenly tumbled backward into the pit with the red hot stones in it. The big creature was badly burned, and the jack-knife position he found himself in made it hard for him to get up.

"Cover him up! Cover him up!" screamed the children, and they quickly buried him with sand and gravel.

When the parents returned to the beach where they had left their children, the giant was dead. "We might not have been here when you came back," the eldest child cried, as all the children ran down to meet their parents' canoe. They all spoke at once. "Big Figure was here!" they said. "We buried him in the cooking pit."

General View of Alert Bay, B.C., Indian Village
Photo Credit: B.C. Provincial Archives

10

Other
People Tales

Wild Man of
the Woods

It happened at the Mahatta Creek when the Sockeye were spawning in the fall. A young man, the son of the chief, was with his family at a fish camp there.

Every morning when it was still dark, the young man would get up. No one else was around. He would go and sit in a pool of ice-cold water with just his head sticking out, until he was numb. That fall the nights were colder and frostier than usual.

The young man wanted to be a strong fighter—better than all the others. He thought the water would make him tough. After sitting in the cold water for a while, he could hardly climb out of the pool and his legs would feel like rubber.

One morning he found that he could not

walk home. His legs would not work properly. While he was struggling to walk, a chipmunk came along with a little flame at the end of its tail. At least, the young man thought it was a little flame. He stumbled after the chipmunk, trying to get close enough to warm himself at the little flame. Then the next thing he knew he was at the top of the big hill behind the fishing camp. He did not know how he got there—he was not himself. He could not remember going up the hill.

He found his legs were working properly by this time, so he started to run down the hill through the thick brush. He could see the roofs of the shelters at the fishing camp and the smoke from the fires. Then suddenly he found that he was at the top of the hill again!

The young man started to run down the hill once more, until he could see the rooftops of his people and the smoke from their campfires. Then he found himself at the top of the hill! Again he could not remember how he got up there.

He decided to try something else. He made a strong rope from boughs of young cedar and tied it around his waist. He planned to run down the hill and, when he got close enough to the camp so that he could see the roofs and smoke, he would quickly tie himself to a tree, then call for help.

So he ran down the steep hill with the rope

tied around his waist. He could hear children playing. Suddenly he was back on top of the hill again!

"I might as well give up and stay here," he thought to himself.

The chief and his wife had been looking for their son. Everyone in the camp looked for him for a long time. Finally they gave up the search. They thought he had been taken by wild animals. When the salmon run was over, the people went back to their village.

A year later when the people returned to the fishing camp, some of the women took a canoe and wandered along the shore. They were approaching a long white beach that looked like a good clamming place.

"What's that on the beach? Is it an eagle?" asked one of the ladies, peering into the distance.

"No, it's too big for an eagle," replied another, "and it hasn't got a white tail and head."

"Maybe it's a bearcub," offered a third woman. "No, I think it's a man," she added as they came closer.

When they were closer yet, the first lady exclaimed, "It's the chief's son who was lost last year!" They could see that it was he, although he had on no clothing and had grown some hair on his body.

The women quietly turned the canoe around.

"We will go back and tell those at the village that we have seen the chief's son," they said.

The next morning the people in the camp all gathered together. "We will take all the canoes and all the men," they decided, "and go quietly along the shore so as not to scare him. If he is clamming on that beach we will sneak behind him and surround him."

Sure enough the young man was digging clams and eating them. He would punch a hole in the shell and suck the contents out.

The people crept up behind him. They were advancing hand in hand and had started to close in on him when he saw them. He jumped up, ran and sprang over the heads of those in the chain. He was a wild man, now. His life in the wilderness had made him very strong and quick. One man saw him disappearing through a hole in the thick bush near a big spruce tree.

The next morning the women of the camp went with the men to try and capture the wild man. This time they would make four lines of people. If he got over the first line maybe one of the other lines would stop him.

It was a beautiful sunny day and again the chief's son was squatting on the beach eating clams. The people sneaked through the trees behind him. "Take it easy," said the leader. "Don't rush. We've got to catch him this time, because if we scare him again he might not come back to this place."

The people, hand in hand, slowly spread out behind Wild Man in four lines. They started closing in. The man who had seen where the wild man had disappeared in the bush the day before hid behind the opening beside the big spruce tree. That man was very nervous.

The four lines of people slowly closed in on Wild Man. He did not notice until they were right behind him. He started up and leaped over the first line, then over the second. The third and fourth lines did not stop him either. He headed toward the spruce tree where the lone man was hiding. All the people watched as Wild Man put his head down and started through the opening in the bushes by the spruce tree.

"I've got him! I'm holding him. Come and help me," cried the lone man. It was just like holding a block of ice.

The others rushed over and helped. They tied the wild man up and took him back to the fishing camp. The chief sent someone ahead of the others to secure his house. They put weights on the roof, supports on the door and tied everything down that was inside.

When Wild Man was brought into the house, they untied him. He would not sit still. His eyes were wild. He paced around and around the house. They gave him food but he would not eat. They gave him the best food they had.

Sockeye salmon, abalone, halibut—he wouldn't even eat tender little clams.

Then Wild Man noticed a red ant crawling up the wall. He picked it off and ate it. That was something he would eat. His family helped him find some more ants.

When he started eating other food, they gave him medicine to bring him back to himself. It was mixed with dry rotten wood and a little salmon. His tongue had shrunk from lack of use, but gradually he was able to speak again.

When he was well, he said to his father, the chief, "I really feel that I am different from all the others. I can jump higher, run faster and am stronger. Now I'm ready to fight." Because of his great strength his tribe won many battles.

The Man with
One Hot Side

According to Mr. Wallas, the man with one hot side came down to the earth at Lawn Point on the northwest coast of Vancouver Island and lived with his tribe there long ago. This story is one told by Mr. Wallas's father.

The people of the village did not know that the man with one hot side was part sunshine. He did not tell them because the villagers seemed to want everybody to be the same. They did not want anyone to have more power than themselves.

One day some people came to the lodge of the man with one hot side and told him that there was a war canoe approaching the village. "It is a big canoe, full of warriors," they shouted.

Hot Side paid little attention. He just said, "Let them come."

Another villager came and told him, "They're coming close to the beach now. You'd better come and hide in the woods. They are here to fight and destroy us."

Hot Side answered, "Don't let it worry you." He gave his son a bow and told him to shoot a wad of shredded cedar bark into the approaching war canoe. When he did so the warriors laughed derisively. So did those watching from their hiding places on shore.

One more attempt was made to convince Hot Side and his family to flee with the others into the thick, tangled forest. "They are landing on the beach now," he was informed. "What are you going to do?"

Hot Side got up off his comfortable bearskin and stretched. He strolled down to the beach and asked the warriors, "What are you up to?"

"We have come to destroy you," they threatened.

"Okay," said Hot Side, "go ahead. I give you the first chance—destroy me."

The warriors picked up their bows and arrows and shot at him but could not seem to wound him.

"You had better stop now," said Hot Side after the men had tried and tried to pierce his flesh with their arrows. "It's my turn now. Let me see what I can do to you."

The warriors did not know what to think. He had no weapon in his hand and their arrows lay spent at his feet. The people of the village watched from their hiding places in the forest. They did not know what was going to happen next.

Suddenly the right side of the man's body lit up like the midday sun while the left side remained as cool as evening. He turned his hot side toward the attackers until the wad of shredded cedar bark caught fire and the canoe began to smoke.

"Don't do it! Don't do it!" the warriors cried in fear, but he continued to direct his hot side toward them. The canoe caught fire, and the warriors jumped to the water but were burned before they reached it. All of them burned as well as their canoe, paddles and weapons.

After that the people of the village no longer laughed at the man with one hot side.

The Fireclub

In the days when there was a lot of fighting for the best locations for fishing camps, this story took place. A young man belonged to a tribe that always seemed to be defeated. A great battle had ensued at his village near Shusharti Bay and there were many dead bodies left lying on the ground.

The wolf always comes around when there has been a battle. He smells the blood from a great distance. "I am going to get power from the wolf," the young man told his parents, "to help us when we fight."

"How are you going to do that?" his father asked.

"Watch what I will do," he said, and when the tide was out he asked his older brother to accompany him to the beach. "Drag me over the barnacles," he instructed, "then put me down where the dead people are."

His brother was not happy but did as he was asked. Searing pain ripped into the young man's back as he was dragged over the barnacles, but he did not flinch. "Now turn me over," he said, "and drag me on my stomach."

His mother and father could not bear to watch when his brother put him, scratched and bleeding, among the dead bodies.

He had not been there long when a big wolf came by, drawn by the smell of fresh blood. The wolf sniffed him, gave him a little push, went away, then came back with another wolf. The young man heard the wolves talking, "This one here must have just died today," one said. "I think he's still breathing," answered the other. The young man held his breath pretending to be dead. The wolves watched him closely. One gave him a push with his elbow.

"He is dead," they finally agreed, and picked him up, one at each end, and carried him away. Every time they jumped over a windfall, the young man took a breath. As they jumped over a big windfall, the wolf that was carrying his feet cried, "I think he's started breathing."

"No, he's dead for sure," responded the other wolf.

After traveling a long time and crossing four

mountains, the wolves neared their home. "Open the door," they shouted. "We are here now." The door was opened and they threw the young man down on the floor.

"My, you picked out a nice fresh one," said an old wolf. "He must have just been killed today. Get the person that butchers the deer—we will have fresh meat tonight."

The deer-cutter came with a big knife. "My, he is fresh," he exclaimed. "We don't often see one that fresh." He raised his knife, but then, the young man jumped to his feet.

"I am alive," he cried. "I came because I want something from you."

"I knew you were alive," stated the old wolf. "I did not say anything because I wanted to see what you would do. What is it you want?"

"We are always defeated when we fight," said the young man. "In the last battle we lost a lot of our people. I don't know if we are poor fighters or if we just have bad luck. I want to get some power from you to help us when we fight."

The wolves admired the young man for his courage and daring. "We will give you what you want," said the head wolf, and went and got his weapons. He selected from them a large club. "This is a club that makes fire," he told the young man. "If you swing it around four times with this side out, it will start a fire. Swing it with the other side out and it will put the fire out. You must look after the club though," the wolf warned, "and do what it says. Hang it on your wall. The club can talk and it will tell you when it wants to go and fight. If you do not listen to it, it will fly off your wall and come back to us."

The young man was grateful. "We can sure use that club," he said. "We have lost too many of our people. I must go back now," he added. "My parents will be worried."

"Some of our wolves will take you back," said the old wolf. "Two will carry you and two will go along in case they need help. It is a long, long way. You have to cross four mountains and cannot find your way alone."

When the young man reached his home, his parents were delighted to see him. When he showed them the club they were anxious to see what it would do. They hung it on their wall as the old wolf had instructed.

One day the club said, "I want to fight," so they took the club out to do battle on their enemies. The young man swung the club four times with the fire side up and their enemies fled before the fire it created.

They had won many battles and controlled the best fishing camps when one day the club said, "I want to fight." But the young man did not listen. He did not feel like fighting that day.

So the club flew off the wall and out the door and headed back to where the wolves dwelled. It stopped to rest on the big mountain at the head of Shusharti Bay and there started a big forest fire. Then it continued on to where the wolves were. You can still see the destruction of that great fire. Trees are just starting to grow back now.

Nighthunter
and Dayhunter

Nighthunter, he who hunts at night, and Dayhunter, he who hunts during the day, were rival hunters. They both provided seal feasts for the people of their villages.

Dayhunter had more power in hunting than Nighthunter had. He found a place where the seal were plentiful. It was the place where they breed in a cave at Dog Island, a small rocky island out from Rumble Beach.

One day he and a companion went out to that island to hunt seal. They did not want other hunters to know of the place, so at half tide they dug a hole on the beach big enough to put their canoe in. They put poles across the canoe and rocks on top of the poles to hold the canoe down when the tide came in.

Dayhunter had to climb down into a rocky

cave on a rope ladder made of twined cedar limbs. His companion stayed at the entrance to the cave as a lookout. That day the lookout saw a man pass by in a canoe but did not think the man saw him.

The man had not seen the lookout but he had seen the submerged canoe. He went back to his village and told some people, "I saw a canoe at Dog Island today."

"Whose was it?" he was asked.

"I don't know. It was submerged and hard to tell," answered the man.

Now Nighthunter had been listening to this conversation and wondered if it could be the canoe of Dayhunter. "I will follow tomorrow," he thought. "Maybe that is where he gets all the seal."

The next day Nighthunter followed Dayhunter's canoe. He stayed a long way behind and when it disappeared from sight he stealthily approached the island. He saw the submerged canoe and brought his own quietly into the bay. Then he sneaked up behind the lookout and killed him with his axe. He threw the lookout and the rope ladder down into the cave so that Dayhunter was trapped.

When Dayhunter discovered his dead companion and the rope ladder on the rocky floor of the cave, he was very frightened. "How will I get out of here?" he wondered. Then he thought, "If I kill enough seal and pile them up, maybe I can climb them to the opening."

But he could not climb the pile of seal. They were so soft and slippery he kept sliding back down.

"Where can I get help?" he thought frantically. He shouted for help and cried and cried. Then it started getting dark in the cave and very cold, so he wrapped his cedar bark blanket around himself and fell asleep on a smooth shelf of rock.

His blanket was over his face when a small voice woke him. "Hey! Don't sleep! Come with me," the small voice said.

He thought he had imagined the voice and was starting to go back to sleep again when he felt something pushing at him. He took the blanket off his face and peered around in the dim light but could see nothing.

Again he tried to go to sleep, this time keeping the blanket off his face. Once more he was disturbed by something nudging him. He looked down and there was a tiny mouse.

"Come with me," the little mouse said. "Follow me and don't let me out of your sight. Follow me close."

So Dayhunter followed the little creature through a long rocky passage. It was very difficult to know where the mouse was leading him because it was so dark.

Finally it started getting lighter and they came upon a big cave where the hunter had never been before. A man sat in the middle of the cave. "I know what has happened to you," the stranger informed him. "I have seen you every time you have come here. You are not going to get help from your people. No one will come for you."

Dayhunter accepted something to eat and a little water to drink from the man. Then he curled up and slept till morning.

When he awoke the strange man was standing before him with a feather cape in his hands. "You will do as I instruct you," said the man, putting on the feathers. He became a loon.

"Climb on to my back under the feathers, and don't put your head out until we surface," continued the loon. The hunter noticed that the loon was taking a sealskin along with them.

He climbed onto the back of the loon and kept his head down under the feathers. They went a long, long way under the water before they surfaced. It was good to see the inlet again.

"Now," said the loon, "we are going to the village of Nighthunter so that you may take revenge on the one who killed your partner and left you to die."

When they approached the village the loon said, "Put this sealskin on and swim behind the island that sits out from the settlement. Just before the tide goes out, show yourself. Pretend that you are half dead."

When the villagers saw him swimming as if he was in a weakened state, they exclaimed, "Hey! Look at the seal out there!" and they ran for their spears.

Nighthunter, who thought himself now to be the greatest seal hunter in the inlet, was the first to take his spear and canoe and go after the seal.

Nighthunter thrust his spear at Dayhunter's cover, but Dayhunter did as the loon had instructed him. He caught the spear and held it to his body, not letting it puncture the skin. Then helped by the force of the outgoing tide, he pulled the canoe down the sound to the open sea.

"When Nighthunter gets worried, he will cut the rope," Loon had said. "But that rope will just stick to the canoe again no matter how many times he cuts it."

Dayhunter pulled Nighthunter to the mouth of the inlet. "It is the first time I have seen a seal so strong," Nighthunter thought. "Usually when you spear a seal it will soon weaken and die."

When they had left the inlet and gone so far out to sea that the mountains on Vancouver Island seemed to submerge, Dayhunter took off the sealskin and said, "You killed my partner and took my hunting ground. Now you can paddle home. I will reach the village easily in this sealskin."

Nighthunter cried out in fear, but Dayhunter swam away and did not look back. When he reached his village he said, "I will never hunt seals in their caves again." He and some of his people went back to Dog Island to get his submerged canoe and to block the entrance to the caves with a big boulder.

A Cannibal Story

A long, long time ago two boys went out hunting deer with their bows and arrows. They went a long way back in the mountains—so far that they were beginning to think they were lost. When they saw a little house with smoke coming from it, they went to the door.

"We were wondering where the best place is to hunt deer," they asked the man that came to the door, "and which is the best way to get back to where we came from."

The man seemed to be very pleased to see them and invited them in the house. "There are a few deer around here," he said. "I can show you the best route to take to your village, but first sit down, and we will cook something for you to eat."

The boys were hungry, so they sat down,

their backs leaning against a board that was propped up on a post. Behind them was a pit where the family made their fires.

The man was building a fire there and putting rocks on it. "When these rocks are red hot, we will cook the food," he said to the boys.

His wife noticed blood on the leg of the younger boy. It was from a scratch he had got going through the brush. She handed him a stick and asked, "Would you scrape that blood off your leg? Our son would like to have it."

So he scraped the blood off his leg and handed the stick back. The little boy licked the blood off the stick with relish, then started chewing the wood.

The visitors looked at each other. The older whispered to the younger, "It looks like it is us that they intend to cook!"

Their host looked up from the fire. "It won't be too long," he smiled. "The rocks are getting hot now."

"Why don't you people sit down here where we are?" suggested one of the boys, getting up. "We'd like to get to know you better."

"Yes," agreed the other boy, rising. "You tell us about this place—how long you've lived here—and we will tell you about the place we come from."

The cannibal and his wife had not talked to anyone for a long time, so they eagerly came around and sat down on the seat. When they were comfortable, their backs leaning against the propped-up board, they started talking. The brothers squatted, facing the cannibals, and joined in the conversation. They could see when the wood of the fire had burned low and the rocks were red hot.

Then one of the boys stood up and yawned and stretched. Suddenly he kicked the post out from behind the board against which the cannibals were leaning. The man and his wife tumbled over backwards into the pit and the boys quickly covered them up with the dirt that had been removed to make the pit. Only the little cannibal was left crouching in a corner.

Just then there was a knock on the door. It was the boys' father, who had been searching for them.

"What are you doing way back here?" their father demanded.

"We were hunting and wandered farther than we intended," answered the older boy.

"I don't like this place," said the father. "I have heard that there are cannibals somewhere in these mountains."

"There are two of them right in there," cried the boys, pointing to the cooking pit. "They are under the earth."

The father turned toward the door, "It is better if you come home now," he said. "You come home now," he repeated.

"Wait, Father," said the older boy. "They should be cooled off now." He started digging where the fire had been. When he reached the remains of the cannibals all that was left of them was very fine ash that flew up in the air. It flew all over the room and out the open door. Anywhere it settled it tried to take blood—and that is how the mosquito came into being.

When the father and his two sons had left that place and were on the trail home, the father said, "Sons, I have never seen a cannibal. You have seen a family of them. When we reach the village you must describe what you have seen, and we will make a mask."

According to Mr. Wallas, the mask is still used today in dances.

The Blind Girl

This story is one that was told by Mr. Wallas's mother. It takes place in the Cape Sutil area where, Mr. Wallas says, a lot of things happened. He remembers a village there where he would go when he was young to camp and fish for halibut.

A young lady, the daughter of the chief of the village, was born blind. She could not see at all. The chief had two servants who would take his daughter where she wanted to go.

One day the blind girl said, "I would like to go to the Cape Scott area. I've never been there before." So she and the two servants went off by canoe.

The chief had a tall totem pole standing beside his fine lodge. There were two eagles that always sat on the totem pole and warned the village if someone approached. From high up on the pole the birds could spot canoes coming long before anyone else. As the blind girl and her two servants moved along in the canoe they could hear the eagles screaming. After a while the blind girl asked, "Will we be there soon? It seems like we have been traveling a long time."

Now the servants that were with the girl had been taken as slaves from another tribe. They had never lost hope of escaping back to their own people and now took the opportunity to try to do so. One of the servants said, "I don't know where we are. It's really foggy here—we seem to be lost."

"Don't worry," said the chief's daughter. "We can turn back now and the eagles' screams will guide us home."

The servants pretended to turn the canoe around but actually headed out to open sea. They paddled and paddled. The blind girl could not tell when night had fallen. When daylight came they could only faintly hear the eagles and by evening of that day they could hear them no longer.

They kept on for two more days. On the evening of the fourth day they reached a strange village. The people of that village met them at the beach and asked, "Where are you from? What are you doing here? You must be from far away—we have not seen canoes like yours before."

"Yes, we come from far away," replied the servants.

"Why did you come here? What do you want?" they were asked. But the servants didn't say much.

One man said to the three, "You'd better come up to the house." He asked the blind girl, "Who are you? What is your name?"

"I am the daughter of a chief," replied the girl. "I don't know how we got here because I can't see. These two servants told me that we were lost in the fog. After two days we could no longer hear the eagles on my father's totem pole. After that we traveled two more days."

"Well, you've come to the right place," said the person who had invited them to his lodge. "I am the chief of this village and I have a son who is of marrying age. You are the daughter of a chief. If you marry my son you may stay here."

Back at the village of the blind girl, her parents were very worried. She had been gone several days and they had not heard of her.

"I fear that our daughter is dead," said the chief to his people. "Perhaps she has drowned, although she had two that can see to help her."

In his grief he ordered, "Fell the totem pole that stands by my lodge for it belonged to my daughter. It will not be raised until I see her again."

When the people cut the tall pole down, it fell into the water toward Hope Island. It is now Nahwitti Bar, a very rough and shallow spot when the tide goes out.

At the strange village, the blind girl married the chief's son and she bore him two strong sons. She waited until their sons were big enough to canoe by themselves and then she told them, "You have grandparents where I come from—I hope they are still alive. Your grandfather was the chief of our village, and I was his only daughter. My father's servants ran away with me one day when they were supposed to take me to Cape Scott. They told me that we were lost in the fog and we ended up here."

"If you find my people," she said to her sons, "and you like it where they are, you may stay."

"We would like to see our grandparents," the boys said. "We will try to find them." So their father made them a sturdy canoe dug out of a cedar tree.

"Paddle south for two days," the mother instructed her sons, "and you will hear the screaming of eagles. Follow the eagles' voices for two more days. When you arrive at the village, tell my father that I am alright. Tell him your names. He will know who you are, for you are named for him." The two sons of the blind lady set off in the canoe their father had made for them. On the second day of their journey they listened for the eagles but could not hear them. They traveled two more days but still did not hear eagles' voices. They soon came to a village and inquired, "In this village is there a chief who once lost a daughter who was blind?" They were told that there was.

"Where is the big house with the totem pole beside it, the house of the chief, our grand-father?" they asked.

"He lives over there in that small house," the man answered. "He took down his big house and the totem pole when his blind daughter did not return."

The boys went to the small house and knocked on the door. Now some of the villagers had been very cruel to the chief when his blind daughter was lost. They would come to his door and say, "Here is your daughter coming— just landing on the beach," or "There is a big canoe approaching. It must be your daughter!" The chief would go out and look, but there would be nothing.

When his grandsons knocked on his door and said who they were, he chased them away. "We have had enough of this," he shouted.

They knocked again at his door and called, "We are your grandsons. Our mother told us your name. She has given us special names so that you will know us."

"You had better go to the door and talk to them," advised the chief's wife.

Finally the chief relented and went to the door. "What are your names?" he asked the boys.

His grandsons told him their names, and the chief knew that they must be the sons of his lost daughter. "Our mother wanted us to come and see you and tell you she is alright," the boys said. They told their grandfather how their mother had been taken away by the servants.

The chief believed them. He knew that they were his grandsons. "Pick up your things," he said to the boys, "and bring them inside."

"Tomorrow we will get the people together and build a fine lodge again. We are going to have a potlatch to celebrate my daughter's safety and that we have two grandsons. We are going to have a big feast and tell the people your names. I feel good now."

Prayer of a Mother
for her Dead Child

"Ah, ah, ah, what is the reason, child, that you have done this to me? I have tried / hard to treat you well when you came to me to have me for your mother. Look at all your toys and all the kinds of things. / What is the reason that you desert me, child? May it be that I did something, child, to you in the way I / treated you, child? I will try better when you / come back to me, child. Please, only become at once well in the place to which you are going. As soon as you are made well, / please, come back to me, child. Please, do not stay away there. / Please, only have mercy on me who is your mother, child," / says she. *

* The Religion of the Kwakiutl Indians, II, page 202.

A Rainbow Gift

Mr. Wallas says that the rainbow belonged to his family on his mother's side and was used by one of his nieces on her infant's grave at the old Quatsino village. It has since been stolen and has been traced, Mr. Wallas believes, to a Vancouver museum.

A chief and his wife, who lived at a camp on the mouth of a river long ago, lost their only son.

They grieved for their child. The father stayed at home but the mother walked alone up the river. She walked and walked, blindly following the river. Then she sat and cried for a while. Then she walked some more.

Night fell. She slept a little, then cried for a while. This went on all night. The next day she walked again. She could not eat. She could not stop grieving for her son. Her heart was broken.

The second night the woman continued to mourn. She sat by the river and cried in the dark.

Suddenly she saw something lighting up the brush near her. It got brighter and lit up the whole thicket. She saw a magnificent rainbow appear in the middle of the light. A man came out of the rainbow and walked toward her.

"What are you doing up the river?" asked the man. "Are you looking for help? I heard you crying. Are you in trouble?"

"Yes," sobbed the woman. "We lost our only son. He is dead."

"Look this way," said the man. "Look closely at the rainbow. When you go home tomorrow you may use this rainbow on your son's grave. It will be for your family's use only, and for their descendants. It will not be used in a dance or for anything except a grave. Go home and tell your husband that I spoke to you and tell him the colors that you saw in the rainbow."

The man and the brilliant rainbow disappeared, but the woman was comforted. When dawn came she went home and told her husband what she had seen and heard.

"I was waiting for you to come back," said her husband. "I thought you might bring something like this."

The man took split cedar boards and made them into a rainbow. He painted them the colors his wife had seen. The little rainbow looked beautiful on their son's small grave. Their hearts were lifted.

Appendix

Concern by Kwakiutl adults that a diminishing number of their young people are able to speak Kwak'wala fluently has caused Kwak'wala language instruction to be instituted into several northern Vancouver Island schools. In conjunction with the Campbell River School District, some of these adults, mostly elderly, have produced alphabet booklets, language lessons, tapes and readers, all of which are available from the Campbell River School District or James Wallas.

Teacher training has also been a part of the program for those Kwakiutl who wished to go into the schools in their areas to teach their language and culture. Mr. Wallas is one of these.

For simplicity's sake the English phonetic-based writing system has been used in this publication. However, for those wishing a more precise knowledge of Kwak'wala, the following material has been included. We gratefully acknowledge the assistance of Peter J. Wilson, linguist, who has compiled this appendix. Peter Wilson has been directly involved in the implementation of the Kwak'wala language instruction program of Vancouver Island.

Pamela M. Whitaker

The appendix presents the $k^wak'^wala$ alphabet, a pronunciation key, and a list of the $k^wak'^wala$ words which appear in the stories. Each alphabet symbol is accompanied by a word to exemplify the sound which the symbol represents. Most words in the alphabet list were suggested by three children who understand a little of the ǧucʼala dialect of $k^wak'^wala$. They are Priscilla Walkus, David Bruce, and Bobby Bruce. They live in Alert Bay with n̓aləsǧəm (Mrs. Alice Peters), who speaks ǧucʼala fluently. The $k^wak'^wala$ words which the children suggest come from the Quatsino, or the Alert Bay - Fort Rupert dialects.

Letter Name and *Example*

Letter	Name	Example	
a	a	da̲	take it
b	b	ba̲ba̲g^{w}əm	boy
c	c	ce̲	to pack water
cˈ	glottolized c	cˈədax̌	woman
d	d	da̲	take it
d^z	d raised z	d^{z}əmid̲^{z}əmi	cat
e	e	ʔe̲	yes
ə	shwa	ʔəm	yes
g	g	gənanəm	child

204

gᵂ	g raised w	gᵂəsu	pig
ǧ	back g	ǧaǧəmp	grandparent
ǧᵂ	back g raised w	ǧᵂadəm	huckleberries
h	h	həmumu	butterfly
i	i	ʔik	good
k	k	kəlxa	car
k'	glottolized k	ƙi	no
kᵂ	k raised w	kᵂixᵂ	eagle
ƙᵂ	glottolized k raised w	ƙᵂaxidəʔs	sit down
l	l	lamadusǧəm	Indian sweater
l'	glottolized l	ləʔəstu	ten
ł	barred l	łəqəstən	seaweed
λ	lambda	ƛabəm	nail
ƛ	barred lambda	ƛħa	to invite people to eat
ƛ'	glottolized barred lambda	ƛ'əwo	oh no
m	m	mayus	raccoon
m'	glottolized m	m'al	sea eggs
n	n	naʔi	snow on ground
n'	glottolized n	n'əm	one
o	o	ʔoligən	wolf
p	p	puxᵂəns	balloon
p'	glottolized p	p'əsp'əyu	ears
q	q	qasa	to walk
qᵂ	q raised w	qᵂəx̌	flour
q'	glottolized q	q'a	to find
qᵂ	glottolized q raised w	q'ᵂəlayu	dear (used to address baby)
s	s	sitəm	snake
t	t	təminəs	squirrel
t'	glottolized t	t'uto	star
u	u	ʔuʔus	bug
w	w	wa	river
w'	glottolized w	w'ac'	dog
x	x	xəndᶻəs	nose
xᵂ	x raised w	xᵂakᵂəna	canoe
x̌	back x	x̌aq	bone
x̌ᵂ	back x raised w	x̌ᵂənukᵂ	daughter or son
y	y	yola	wind
y'	glottolized y	y'aksəm	bad
ʔ	glottol stop	ʔaʔən	eyebrow
∕	stress mark		the stress mark is used to indicate the main or primary stress in the word.

Pronunciation Key

There are forty-eight distinct sounds in K^wak'^wala, forty-two consonants and six vowels. The vowels follow the International Phonetic Alphabet values, which are similar to the sounds the vowels represent in French, for example.

a   as in f*a*ther
i   as in m*ee*t
u   as in b*oo*t
o   as in b*oa*t
e   as in w*ei*ght
ə   as in b*u*t

The consonants *p t m n l w s b d h* represent the same sounds they do in English. The symbols *k* and *g* represent sounds that are similar to their English counterparts but sound as though they are followed by a *y* (as in *yes*) — thus *ky* and *gy*, respectively. The *c* sounds as *ts*, and *d^z* as *dz*.

The symbols which are followed by a raised *w* are pronounced with rounded lips and sound to English speakers as though they are followed by a *w*. The symbols which are accompanied by a raised ' are glottolized, e.g.: *k'*, glottolized *k*. These sounds are harder and click-like compared to their non-glottolized counterparts.

The symbols λ, $\hat{\lambda}$ and $\hat{\lambda}'$ sound like *gl*, *kl*, and *k'l*, respectively.

The symbol *x* represents a sound which was lost from English around the time of the Norman Conquest but is still present in our spelling, e.g.: as the *gh* in li*gh*t and ri*gh*t.

The word *loch* in German, meaning "hole," is pronounced with a final *x*.

The symbol *x^w* represents a sound which is produced by rounding the lips and blowing out an unsuccessful whistle.

The symbol ⱡis pronounced by placing the tongue on the roof of the mouth and blowing out on both sides.

The sounds which are represented by *q q' q^w q'^w* X̣ and X̣^w are quite difficult to pronounce. The *q* series is similar to the *k'* series but is produced farther back in the mouth. The X̣ and X̣^w are similar to the *x* and *x^w* described earlier, but are pronounced farther back in the mouth.

The ʔ sounds like the stop in the middle of the negative expression uh-uh.

People and Places

Kwakiutl	kʷaguƚ	a people
Kwak'wala	kʷak'ʷala	the language of the kʷaguƚ
Quatsino	ǧúsgimukʷ	Quatsino people
The Quatsino dialect of Kwak'wala	ǧu'cala	
Cash Creek (Shuttleworth Bight)	gusəʔe	place where the gusgimukʷ came from
Those who remained at gusəʔe	nəqəmgəlisa	always stay in the same place
Tribe at Hope Island	ƛ̓aƛ̓asikʷəla	
Village at Hope Island	x̌ʷəmdasbe	
Village on Quatsino Sound	x̌ʷətis	

James Wallas's Forefathers

Father (Jimmy Jumbo)	n'an'əmugʷidᶻal'əs	from x̌ʷətis
Mother (Jeanny Jumbo)	ƛil'inux̌ʷ	from x̌ʷəmdasbe
Paternal Grandfather	n'an'əmugʷidᶻal'əs	from x̌ʷətis
Paternal Grandmother	weƛilay'ugʷa	from x̌ʷətis
Maternal Grandfather	ƛ̓aqʷagila	from x̌ʷəmdasbe
Maternal Grandmother	maxʷməwidᶻəmǧa	from x̌ʷəmdasbe

bədí	- cougar
bə́k'ʷəs	- wild man - man in the woods
bə́lǧina	- a small whale (not a gray whale, although it is gray colored)
cáx̌is	- Beaver Harbour - to go along the beach in a trotting motion (similar to a duck)
c'aw	- beaver

cᶜəlqʷal'uλəla	- to be getting heat
c'igis	- to lie on beach or in deep water looking up with leer on face - like a huge bullhead
daⁱtdaⁱta	- spreading - that can be spread
d axʷən	- eulachon or oolachan
dᶻúnuq'ẅa	- woods giant
ǧəmút'ala	- the sound of a wolf howling
ǧənəm	- wife
ǧúsəʔe	- Cash Creek (Shuttleworth Bight)
ǧúsgimukʷ	- Quatsino people
ǧʷa, ǧʷa, ǧʷa	- qa, qa, qa, the raven's cry
ǧʷáləs	- lizard - the period that he stopped in
ǧʷaw'ina	- raven
ǧʷəl'ik	- pitch (man) in story
hanaλəʔenuxʷ	- hunter
hənx̌əstalis	- to look at reflection in water
hə́nx̌a	- to look into mirror - to look for self on bottom of water
kos	- blow hole
k̓úlis	- big blue whale
k'ədəláwi	- kingfisher
kʷənxʷa	- thunder (bird) in story
kʷikʷ	- eagle
k'ʷix̌agila	- someone who knows how to make plans - raven
λ́asǧas	- Klaskish - a place that is outside
λ́asqinuxʷ	- Klakish people - people that live at a place that is outside
λáλəny'əm	- baby black bear
λ̓e	- black bear
λ̓əwəls	- elk
λⁱin'a	- olachon oil

208

ƛisəlagil'əkʷ	- made like the sun
ƛisəla	- the sun
maxʔenuxʷ	- killer whale
məládi	- Mahatta - a place that has sockeye
migʷat	- seal
m'əkʷəla	- moon
nikʷiƛagəmi	- nighthunter
n'e ƛagəmi	- dayhunter
n'əmugʷis	- This word is used to describe a person who is left alone on the beach. It is used as the kwak'wala title of the book.
p'əp'as	- blind
q'ánəs	- chiton
q'an'iqel'əkʷ	- creator - transformer - made so that he could soar
q'an'i	- to soar
q'ʷac'əq	- snail (long—6"—slug-like snail)
q'wəláʔsta	- life giving liquid
sisiyuƛ	- double headed serpent or snake
siɫəm	- snake, serpent
tak'us	- deer
t'ubiw'a	- fawn (refers to the spots)
t'up'əy'ac'i	- flea
w'áləs	- big (in kwak'wala). This is the origin of Wallas's name.
w'ac'	- dog (singular)
w'əʔoc'i	- dogs (plural)
xaxəmalagila	- bastard maker
xʷat'əs	- wren
xʷəmduma	- land otter
ʔaba ƛ'a	- woods giant's woman
ʔəwik'ədz	- Calvert Island
ʔul'igən	- wolf

Gwayasdums Village, 1900
Photo: Royal B.C. Museum

Spirit Hawk Mask
Museum of Man -- Ottawa

Quatsino Woman
Photo: Museum of Man - Ottawa

Kwakiutl Dance to Restore Eclipsed Moon
Photo: Edward S. Curtis

INDIAN TITLES

Ah Mo
Tren J. Griffin
ISBN 0-88839-244-3

American Indian Pottery
Sharon Wirt
ISBN 0-88839-134-X

Argillite: Art of the Haida
Drew & Wilson
ISBN 0-88839-037-8

Art of the Totem
Marius Barbeau
ISBN 0-88839-168-4

Coast Salish
Reg Ashwell
ISBN 0-88839-009-2

Eskimo Life Yesterday
Hancock House
ISBN 0-919654-73-8

Haida: Their Art & Culture
Leslie Drew
ISBN 0-88839-132-3

Hunter Series
By R. Stephen Irwin, MD
Hunters of the Buffalo
ISBN 0-88839-176-5

Hunters of the E. Forest
ISBN 0-88839-178-1

Hunters of the Ice
ISBN 0-88839-179-X

Hunters of the N. Forest
ISBN 0-88839-175-7

Hunters of the Sea
ISBN 0-88839-177-3

Images: Stone: BC
Wilson Duff
ISBN 0-295-95421-3

The Incredible Eskimo
de Coccola & King
ISBN 0-88839-189-7

Indian Art & Culture
Kew & Goddard
ISBN 0-919654-13-4

Indian Artifacts of the NE
Roger W. Moeller
ISBN 0-88839-127-7

Indian Coloring Books
Carol Batdorf

Seawolf
ISBN 0-88839-247-8

Tinka
ISBN 0-88839-249-4

Indian Healing
Wolfgang G. Jilek, MD
ISBN 0-88839-120-X

Indian Herbs
Dr. Raymond Stark
ISBN 0-88839-077-7

Indian Hunters
R. Stephen Irwin, MD
ISBN 0-88839-181-1

Indian Quillworking
Christy Ann Hensler
ISBN 0-88839-214-1

Indian Rock Carvings
Beth Hill
ISBN 0-919654-34-7

Indian Tribes of the NW
Reg Ashwell
ISBN 0-919654-53-3

Indian Weaving, Knitting
& Basketry of the NW
Elizabeth Hawkins
ISBN 0-88839-006-8

Iroquois: Their Art & Crafts
Carrie A. Lyford
ISBN 0-88839-135-8

Kwakiutl Legends
Chief Wallas & Whitaker
ISBN 0-88839-094-7

Life with the Eskimo
Hancock House
ISBN 0-919654-72-X

More Ahmo
Tren J. Griffin
ISBN 0-88839-303-2

My Heart Soars
Chief Dan George
ISBN 0-88839-231-1

My Spirit Soars
Chief Dan George
ISBN 0-88839-233-8

NW Native Harvest
Carol Batdorf
ISBN 0-88839-245-1

Power Quest
Carol Batdorf
ISBN 0-88839-240-0

River of Tears
Maud Emery
ISBN 0-88839-276-1

Spirit Quest
Carol Batdorf
ISBN 0-88839-210-9

Tlingit
Dan & Nan Kaiper
ISBN 0-88839-010-6

Totem Poles of the NW
D. Allen
ISBN 0-919654-83-5

Western Indian Basketry
Joan Megan Jones
ISBN 0-88839-122-6

When Buffalo Ran
George Bird Grinnell
ISBN 0-88839-258-3

ESKIMO TITLES

Eskimo Life Yesterday
Hancock House
ISBN 0-919654-73-8

The Incredible Eskimo
de Coccola & King
ISBN 0-88839-189-7

Life with the Eskimo
Hancock House
ISBN 0-919654-72-X